PASSAGE
TO THE
GOLDEN GATE

A History of the Chinese in America to 1910

Daniel Chu and
Samuel Chu, Ph.D.

Illustrated by Earl Thollander

ZENITH BOOKS
DOUBLEDAY & COMPANY, INC., GARDEN CITY, NEW YORK

Lines from "Truthful James"
from THE BEST OF BRET HARTE
edited by Wilhelmina Harper and Aimee Peters
and published by the Houghton Mifflin Company.

The Zenith Books edition, published simultaneously in hardbound
and paperback volumes, is the first publication of PASSAGE TO THE
GOLDEN GATE.

Zenith Books edition: 1967

The aim of Zenith Books is to present the history of minority groups in the United States and their participation in the growth and development of the country. Through histories and biographies written by leading historians in collaboration with established writers for young people, Zenith Books will increase the awareness of minority group members of their own heritage and at the same time develop among all people an understanding and appreciation of that heritage.

Dr. John Hope Franklin, currently Professor of History at the University of Chicago, has also taught at Brooklyn College, Fisk University, and Howard University. For the year 1962–63, he was William Pitt Professor of American History and Institutions at Cambridge University in England. He is the author of many books, including FROM SLAVERY TO FREEDOM, THE MILITANT SOUTH, RECONSTRUCTION AFTER THE CIVIL WAR, and THE EMANCIPATION PROCLAMATION.

Shelley Umans is a specialist in reading instruction and is a member of the instructional staff of Teachers College, Columbia University. For more than ten years, she has been a consultant to many major urban school systems throughout the United States. She is the author of NEW TRENDS IN READING INSTRUCTION, DESIGNS FOR READING PROGRAMS, and co-author of TEACHING THE DISADVANTAGED.

Daniel Chu is an editor with Scholastic Magazines. He has written extensively for junior and senior high school students, and is the co-author of another Zenith Book, A GLORIOUS AGE IN AFRICA.

Dr. Samuel Chu is an Associate Professor of History at the University of Pittsburgh. He is responsible for East Asian Studies in the social sciences and specializes in modern Chinese history.

Earl Thollander studied art at the City College of San Francisco and received a B.A. degree from the University of California at Berkeley. As an illustrator of numerous children's books and cookbooks, he has made special trips to various parts of the world to obtain material for his drawings and paintings. Some of the books he has illustrated include RAMON MAKES A TRADE, TO CATCH A MONGOOSE, and THE 1000 RECIPE CHINESE COOK BOOK.

Other Outstanding Zenith Books

FOUR TOOK FREEDOM, by Philip Sterling and Rayford Logan. The lives of Harriet Tubman, Frederick Douglass, Robert Smalls, and Blanche K. Bruce.

A GLORIOUS AGE IN AFRICA, by Daniel Chu and Elliott Skinner. The story of three great African empires.

GREAT RULERS OF THE AFRICAN PAST, by Lavinia Dobler and William A. Brown, with special consultant Philip Curtin. Five African rulers who led their nations in times of crisis.

A GUIDE TO AFRICAN HISTORY, by Basil Davidson, revised and edited by Haskel Frankel. A general survey of the African past from earliest times to the present.

LIFT EVERY VOICE, by Dorothy Sterling and Benjamin Quarles. The lives of W. E. B. Du Bois, Mary Church Terrell, Booker T. Washington, and James Weldon Johnson.

PIONEERS AND PATRIOTS, by Lavinia Dobler and Edgar A. Toppin. The lives of six Negroes of the colonial and revolutionary eras.

TIME OF TRIAL, TIME OF HOPE, by Milton Meltzer and August Meier. The history of the Negro in America from 1919 to 1941.

THE UNFINISHED MARCH, by Carol Drisko and Edgar A. Toppin. The Negro in the United States from Reconstruction to World War I.

WORTH FIGHTING FOR, by Agnes McCarthy and Lawrence Reddick. A history of the Negro in the United States during the Civil War and Reconstruction.

CONTENTS

CHAPTER ONE

CHINA CLIPPERS

An American sailing ship named the *Empress of China* worked her way up the Pearl River and dropped anchor in the port of Canton. The year was 1784. A 360-tonner from New York, she was the first ship flying the American flag to reach a Chinese port.

The arrival of Americans at Canton (pronounced can-tong) apparently caused little excitement in China. But the event meant a great deal to the then struggling young nation called the United States of America.

The American Revolutionary War had ended scarcely two years earlier. Thirteen former British colonies in North America had fought for their independence and won.

Victory, however, brought new problems. Among other things, the Revolutionary War had disrupted the old patterns of American trade with other lands. The break from Great Britain had closed the profitable British West Indies trade to American shipping. This trade was mainly an exchange of American farm and forest products for West Indian sugar and molasses. It had been important for the growth and prosperity of the leading American ports, especially the ports of New England.

Unless new markets were found for American products—and found quickly—the young American nation faced the possibility of financial ruin.

Yankee seafaring men boldly took up the challenge. They sailed off to distant places, sometimes without even maps and charts to guide them. Picking up an item in one place to exchange for something else in another place, they traded whatever, whenever, and wherever they could.

Perhaps the most ambitious effort to set up new trade links was started by a group of New York merchants. In 1783, this group fitted out an ex-Revolutionary War privateer. They renamed the ship the *Empress of China*, and sent her off to Canton for the purpose of "commerce with the Chinese Empire."

From this rather uncertain beginning, America's China trade picked up rapidly. By 1789, as many as fifteen American-flag ships could be seen crowded into the Canton harbor at one time. They came there from Boston, Salem, Providence, New York, Philadelphia, Baltimore, and other leading seaports of the U. S. Atlantic coast.

The main item for which American shipmasters sailed halfway around the world was tea. Since tea drinking had long become an established custom in much of Europe and America, there was always a ready market for tea—and a large profit for every shipment brought back from China.

Other important items from the China trade included silk, porcelain tableware (which came to be called "chinaware," or sometimes just plain "china"), nankeen (a cotton cloth used in those days for men's trousers), and various art and furniture objects produced by skilled Chinese workmen and craftsmen from ivory, jade, bronze, copper, and lacquered wood.

But if the Yankee shipmasters knew what they wanted from China, they had a harder time finding items the Chinese would need and want in return. After trying one thing and another, American shipowners discovered several luxury items that the Chinese seemed to want in great amounts. These included furs (especially of seals and sea otters), sandalwood (a sweet smelling tropical wood sometimes burned as an incense in Chinese temples and homes), and *bêche-de-mer* (commonly called "sea cucumbers," an ugly sea animal that the Chinese considered delicious when cooked in soups and other dishes). This highly unusual cargo resulted in a complicated trade route. As pioneered by Boston shipmasters, it generally followed this route:

New England merchants loaded their sailing vessels with metal tools, mirrors, and various other knickknacks. The ships sailed down the Atlantic coast of the Americas, around the tip of South America, and back up the Pacific coast. Eventually arriving in the Pacific Northwest, the ships put into Nootka Sound to exchange their cargo for sea-otter furs collected by the Indians of Vancouver Island.

After that the ships set sail across the Pacific. They might pay a call at the Hawaiian Islands to pick up a load of sandalwood and perhaps stop at the East Indies for *bêche-de-mer* before heading for China.

On arriving in Canton, the cargoes picked up along

Trade Route to the Orient

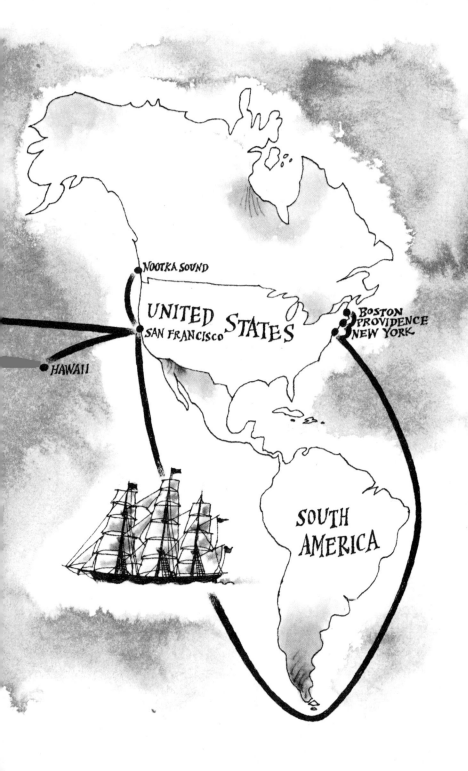

the way would be traded for Chinese goods. Finally, the ships would begin their homeward voyage, often returning by way of the Indian Ocean, around the tip of Africa, and across the Atlantic Ocean to make one complete trip around the world.

For those American sailing men, a China trade voyage meant more than a year spent on the high seas. It was not unusual for such sailing trips, including all stopovers, to last up to three years. But the profits of the China trade made it well worth the time and risks. Trade with China created private fortunes for many merchant, banking, and shipowning families in New England and along the Atlantic seaboard. It brought good times to American port cities. The young United States moved back from the edge of national ruin and onto a firmer financial footing.

The China trade also had an important side effect. The route of the China traders gave Americans their first good look at the Pacific side of the North American continent. In 1792 a Boston ship, the *Columbia,* sailed up a broad river in the Pacific Northwest. The river was promptly named the Columbia River, after the visiting ship. It was because of this visit that the United States later claimed the land through which the Columbia River flowed—an area that came to be known as Oregon Country.

Actually, Americans were latecomers to the China trade scene. The Portuguese had reached Canton as early as the year 1516. Dutch merchantmen had first put into the port off the South China Sea in 1624, and were followed by the English in 1637. Soon thereafter nearly every European maritime nation set up trade with China.

Curiously enough, the people that seemed to be least interested in the China trade were the Chinese themselves.

China—the "Celestial Empire"—was seen by its own people as a world of its own, needing help from no one. The Chinese tended to regard all outsiders as barbarians. And the Imperial government of China wanted as little to do with barbarians as possible. It opened one —and only one—Chinese port to foreign traders. That port was the southern Chinese city of Canton.

In 1793, Britain's King George III sent the Earl of Macartney to China to see about a new commercial treaty. The British wanted to expand their China trade and to open other Chinese ports to British ships. But the Emperor of China, Ch'ien-lung, told the British envoy:

"The Celestial Empire possesses all things in prolific abundance and lacks no products within its borders. There is therefore no need to import the manufactures of outside barbarians in exchange for our own products."

The Emperor made it very clear that his government in leaving the port of Canton open to foreign trade was being generous enough.

By the time the Americans began to take part in the China trade in earnest, the Canton system was already firmly set up. All foreign ships entering the mouth of the Canton River had to stop first at Macao, a Portuguese settlement on the south China coast some eighty-five miles downstream from Canton. (Macao, pronounced mah-cow, remains to this day a Portuguese-ruled city.)

At Macao, the foreign ship was issued a "chop" (or permit with an official seal). This permitted it to go farther up the river for search and inspection by Chinese officials. Then the ship sailed up the Pearl River to Whampoa Island. There, it dropped anchor and moved its cargo to smaller river boats for the last twelve miles to Canton.

On landing, foreign trading activities were kept to an area about a half-mile square just outside the walled city of Canton. Here there were thirteen large "factory buildings" in a row along a street named, not very surprisingly, Thirteen Factory Street. These were not actually factories as such. They were a combination of warehouses, offices, and apartments for foreign traders. Each of the buildings was owned by a different foreign country—their ownership clearly identified by their national flags flying out front.

The foreign trader in Canton had little contact with the Chinese people. All business was carried on with a small group of Chinese known as the Hong merchants. Foreigners were made to observe strict rules of behavior while in China. Among other things, they were not allowed to go into the city of Canton itself. Nor were they permitted to travel in groups of more than ten persons at a time. If any of them ever thought of going rowing on the Pearl River, they could forget it. That was against the rules, too.

The tight rules irritated the foreign traders. The Chinese, on their part, resented the refusal of the foreign visitors to obey Chinese laws. The Westerners refused to accept the Chinese laws because they thought the penalties of Chinese criminal law far too severe.

Thus, it was only a matter of time before the resentment between foreigners and Chinese boiled over. When the conflict came, it was centered on an argument over bringing opium into China.

Opium smoking, like taking many other narcotics, tends to be habit forming. Opium addiction is extremely harmful to the human body. Though opium addiction was not a particularly serious problem in China before 1800, the habit increased alarmingly from the 1800s on. By the 1830s, an estimated two to ten million Chinese were addicted to the drug.

Practically all the opium consumed in China was imported by foreigners. The traders of many nations engaged in the drug traffic. But the opium trade was largely controlled by British merchants who had easy access to opium poppies grown in Bengal in the then British-controlled India.

The Chinese government had tried to outlaw the shipment of opium into China. It was not very successful. Enterprising foreign merchants, helped by corrupt Chinese officials and smugglers, kept the harmful drug flowing into Canton. The opium traffic brought enormous profits to the foreign merchants, and their greed for its profits proved stronger than their sense of right and wrong.

Finally, in 1838, the Chinese government began to take strong steps to stamp out the opium evil. The death penalty was decreed for all (including foreigners) who grew, sold, or smoked opium. The government seized and destroyed all opium shipments to Canton.

Bad feelings mounted between the Chinese and the British. In November 1839, Chinese war junks and British warships engaged in a pitched battle off Canton. So began the Anglo-Chinese war—often called the Opium War.

The following summer, a British force of seventeen warships, twenty-seven troop ships, and four thousand soldiers arrived on the China scene. And from that point on, it was hardly a contest. China's military forces were no match for the superior industrial and military technology of the West. For the badly organized, ill-equipped Chinese forces, defeat followed dreary defeat.

In the Nanking Treaty of 1842 ending the Opium War, the Chinese bowed to a number of British demands. The island of Hong Kong off the China coast was given to Britain (Hong Kong is still a British colony). The Chinese also agreed to open four other ports in addition to Canton to foreign trade. These four ports were Amoy, Foochow, Ningpo, and Shanghai.

The China trade was always highly competitive among the many foreign traders. The other foreign merchants were not about to let their British competitors hold a trade advantage over them for long. A treaty in 1844 gave French merchants the same privileges won by the British in the Opium War. In the same year the United States gained similar trade and residence rights in China for Americans.

With the opening of the new treaty ports in China, the tea trade hit boom proportions again. The China traders soon realized that speed on the high seas would give them an edge over rivals in the tea business. The result was the building of a fleet of swift sailing ships—the famous China tea clippers.

From the drawing boards of such brilliant American naval architects as John W. Griffiths, Samuel H. Pook, and Donald McKay came the designs for the tall, slender, sleek clipper ships which raced around the world, breaking speed records as they went. The Griffiths-designed clipper *Rainbow* completed a round trip voyage to China in 1846 in just seven months and seventeen days, including all stopovers, delays, and time spent loading and unloading cargo. In 1851 the McKay-designed *Flying Cloud,* possibly the most famous clipper of them all, made its first China trade voyage. On the first leg of the trip, she made the fifteen-thousand-mile run from New York around South America to San Francisco in eighty-nine days and twenty-one hours, a record never beaten by any other sailing ship.

These beautiful China clippers wrote the last glamorous and exciting chapter to the days of the sailing vessels. Already, they were being challenged by new steam-driven ships. But the drama, the excitement, and the beauty of these tall-masted, full-rigged clippers would stay on in the memories of seafaring men long after the clipper ships had disappeared from the high seas.

The opening of the new treaty ports and the increase in shipping traffic across the Pacific encouraged more American traders, as well as educators and Christian missionaries, to cross the ocean and see China for themselves. At the same time, a trickle of Chinese began to arrive on American shores.

With the opening of the new treaty ports in China, the tea trade hit boom proportions again.

No one really knows when the Chinese first came to the New World. Some historians have said there is evidence of the presence of Chinese on the Pacific coast in the 16th, 17th, and 18th centuries (indeed, even before the Spanish and Americans arrived there). Tradition has it that the first Chinese to reach the Pacific coast were two men and one woman. They accompanied an American merchant named Charles V. Gillespie to San Francisco aboard the American brig *Eagle* in 1848.

Other records claim even earlier trips to the East coast. They say that there was a handful of Chinese visitors in New England during the late 1700s and perhaps a half-dozen Chinese students in Connecticut in the early 1800s. More reliable records report the arrival of three Chinese boys to study at Monson Academy in Massachusetts in 1847. One of them, Yung Wing, later went on to Yale to become the first Chinese to earn a degree from an American university.

In any event, there were very few Chinese in America during the first fifty years of the 19th century. The United States territorial census of 1830, for example, could find only three Chinese to count. By 1840, that number had risen to eight.

But an event occurred in 1848 which would draw Chinese by the thousands across the ocean to America. It was the same event which drew many thousands of people from many parts of the world to California: the discovery of gold at a place called Sutter's Mill.

CHAPTER TWO

GOLD FEVER

It all started when a man called Sutter decided to build a new sawmill.

This particular Sutter was John Augustus Sutter, one of the early settlers of California. Born in Germany of Swiss parents, he came to America in 1834. During his first years in America, Sutter supported himself as a trader in Missouri. Soon he grew restless and decided to move on to the Pacific coast. He made his way along the Oregon Trail to the Pacific Northwest. Sutter eventually wound up in a Pacific coastal village called Yerba Buena in 1839.

In a few years, Yerba Buena would grow and become the city of San Francisco. But when Sutter arrived there, it was still just a small, plain village in Alta California (Upper California), at that time a province of Mexico. (California did not become a part of the United States until 1848.)

Happily, John Augustus Sutter became great friends with the Mexican governor of Alta California. At Sutter's request, the governor granted him forty-nine thousand acres for a settlement.

Sutter hired two small boats and worked his way up the Sacramento River to his land grant. There he founded his settlement in the Sacramento Valley and named it New Helvetia (New Switzerland) in honor of the homeland of his parents.

In effect, New Helvetia turned into Sutter's private kingdom. He built a good-sized fort near the spot where the American River joined the Sacramento River. When American pioneers began to wander into Alta California during the 1840s, Sutter—a generous man—let the newcomers use his fort as a way station and place of refuge.

Sutter's holdings prospered. On the rich, rolling land he planted wheat and other grains. Some of the land was given over to fruit orchards, or used as grazing fields for his huge herds of cattle. Yet, the land proved even richer than Sutter had imagined.

In 1847, Sutter decided to build a sawmill at Coloma on the south fork of the American River. Coloma was forty or so miles upriver from a new settlement called Sacramento City. He turned over the job to one of his employees, a carpenter named James W. Marshall. And it was on January 24, 1848, that Marshall, while working around the new sawmill, noticed bits of golden metal flashing in the millpond.

Marshall picked up some of the metal. It looked like gold. He pounded the metal with a rock. The metal flattened like gold. It *was* gold!

Four days and forty miles later, Marshall burst into his employer's office at Sutter's Fort and excitedly reported his find. Sutter was not overjoyed at hearing the news. He seemed deeply troubled. He begged Marshall and his other employees who knew about the find to keep the discovery quiet for a while. Sutter felt that the news of the find would bring hordes of gold-hungry men trampling into his lands to destroy his dream for New Helvetia.

John Augustus Sutter was so right!

The news spread. Large numbers of gold-hungry men came. The trespassers slaughtered Sutter's cattle without asking him. Their grazing horses ruined his grain fields. They stole from him at every opportunity. Sutter tried to make the best of it. But, in time, the outsiders drove him from his own land. (Sutter eventually left California to live out his last years in Pennsylvania. He died in 1880.)

The discovery of gold at Sutter's Mill in 1848 helped to change the course of California's history. It touched off the world's first great gold rush.

Gold fever swept California. Towns and villages quickly emptied as their inhabitants rushed off to the hills to dig for gold. As a San Francisco newspaper owner sadly reported: "The majority of our subscribers and many of our advertisers have closed their doors and places of business and left town. . . ." Whereupon, the publisher himself gave in to the hunger for gold and left town to join his former subscribers and advertisers in their search for gold.

In time, the news spread to the eastern United States —and then across the Atlantic to Europe—causing great excitement everywhere. Men by the tens of thousands (the exact number can only be guessed at) hastily left farms, homes, and jobs to make their way, in one way

It is said that the first Chinese to reach the Pacific coast were two men and one woman. They sailed into San Francisco Bay on the American brig Eagle.

or another, to the Golden Gate on the Pacific coast. They went to California in such huge numbers during the year 1849 that they have become permanently known in American lore as the Forty-Niners.

Eventually, the news of the California gold find reached China. In countless villages around the city of Canton, stories were told of a place where gold was just laying around for anybody to come along and scoop it up. (The stories became exaggerated as they were told and retold). And in these countless villages, countless young men began to dream of going to this fabulous place which, in the language of the Cantonese, came to be called *Gum San*—the land of the Golden Mountains.

During the first fifty years of the 19th century, the laws of the Chinese Imperial government were quite clear on the matter of leaving the country: no Chinese could leave China.

This, however, was a law that the Chinese government could not and did not enforce very strictly.

In reality, the Chinese had been emigrating to the lands of Southeast Asia for centuries—to Burma, Siam (now called Thailand), Vietnam, Malaya, the Philippines, and elsewhere. But it was in the late 1840s that the number of Chinese who left China for foreign lands showed a sharp increase. It was then that a so-called "coolie" trade developed.

The word "coolie" may have come from "kuli," a term used in British India to describe a burden bearer (in the sense of an unskilled laborer). It happens that two Chinese words that sound very much like "ku" and "li" translate to mean "bitter strength" or "bitter work." It was a good description of the hard life of the Chinese manual laborer. Regardless of how the word began, "coolie" came to mean a Chinese manual laborer.

There were three main reasons for the development of the coolie trade. First, a world-wide trend toward the abolition of slavery had created a need for a new kind of cheap labor. Second, the increase in the number of ships in the South China Sea made it easy to ship Chinese workers to such places as the Malayan peninsula, Singapore, Java, or to places farther away from China such as Hawaii, Cuba, and Peru. Third, China, with its huge number of poor people, could supply this labor demand, and Chinese coolie traders did just that.

In practice, the overseas Chinese coolie trade was a type of debt bondage not too different from the indentured servant system familiar in America during its own colonial times. The workings of the coolie trade varied with time and place. But it followed a basic pattern. It began with a need for cheap labor to develop new farms and plantations in different parts of the world. Coolie traders recruited laborers in the cities and villages of China. They then arranged their transportation to where they were needed.

Almost without exception, the Chinese laborers recruited for work abroad came from very poor peasant families. It was rare to find one who could pay his own passage overseas. Most of the laborers recruited in this way went deeply into debt to the coolie traders through a kind of "go now, pay later" plan known as the credit-ticket system.

Under this system, the coolie traders loaned the passage money to the recruited laborers. The loans, plus interest, were to be paid back later out of the workers' earnings abroad. This usually worked out like an installment loan: a certain amount was taken from each paycheck until the debt was paid off in full. Because these poor laborers had no other way to finance their passage to another country, the coolie traders often charged unfair interest rates and added on all sorts of extra charges for real or imagined services.

The coolie trade, then, was a business dealing in the ability of human beings to perform work. At its worst, when the laborers were often kidnaped, the coolie trade was only a step away from a form of slavery.

Yet most of the Chinese laborers who became part of the coolie trade did so by choice. This raises the question of why anyone would of his own choice leave his home and family and go off to some faraway land for what he knew would be long years of hard and unending labor.

To understand the reasons which caused these Chinese to follow such a drastic course, we have to know something about the land that was their home, the society into which they were born, and the hopes and goals they set for themselves.

CHAPTER THREE

THE SOJOURNERS' DREAM

More than half of all the Chinese who left China during the 19th century (and nearly all the Chinese who were to emigrate to America in those times) came from a single Chinese province. This was the province of Kwangtung in southern China.

A key reason for this was the special role played by the city of Canton, Kwangtung's capital. Canton, remember, was for many years the only Chinese seaport open to foreign trade. Even after the Opium War, when the four other Chinese ports were opened to trade, Canton remained the major place for Chinese-foreign contacts.

The Chinese who came from Kwangtung probably would describe themselves, in a single word, as "Cantonese." Actually, the society of the Cantonese was somewhat more complicated than that.

Kwangtung's topography contains almost everything: mountains and misty river valleys, windswept plateaus, lowlands and shoreside mud flats. For the purposes of local administration, the province was divided into some ninety individual districts.

Most of the districts were rural. The people lived in countless farming towns and small villages. They worked mainly in growing rice or mulberry bushes and practicing silk culture (silkworms producing this prized fiber find mulberry leaves especially tasty). Many kinds of fruits—pineapples, oranges, peaches, pears, mangoes, and litchis—were grown in the hillier regions.

Kwangtung also had a number of crowded cities. The largest of these, of course, was Canton. In those days, Canton was surrounded by a high wall. Within the wall was a mass of low, tiled-roof houses and narrow, twisting streets wandering in all directions. All the different things that made up the complex world of Kwangtung could be found in the hustle and bustle of its main city Canton. The Pearl River Delta including Canton and some one hundred miles around was one of the most crowded places on earth.

Unfortunately, this was also a strangely quarrelsome world. For as long as anyone could remember, villages fought with neighboring villages, mountaineers with lowlanders, peasants with city folks. Sometimes the fights grew into local wars in which villages were burned and hundreds of people killed.

Many problems split the world of Kwangtung. In part, the conflicts reflected differences among three very different groups of people who lived in this region.

The first group described themselves as *Punti*, or "natives." They were descendants of native Cantonese. These people had lived in this part of China for as long as anyone could remember.

The second group was the *Hakka*, or "strangers," a people from the northeastern provinces of China. They

Problems split the world of Kwangtung. Three very different groups of people—Hakka, Punti, and Tanka—found it difficult to live in peace.

began moving into the Kwangtung regions about the 13th century. Generally the Puntis and Hakkas did not get along. One problem was they hardly even spoke the same language and had trouble understanding each other. Hakkas spoke their own dialect (a dialect is a spoken variation of the same language) which was a little like the Mandarin Chinese spoken in North China. The Puntis, on the other hand, spoke the local dialect of Cantonese (some language experts do not consider Cantonese a dialect but an entirely separate language from Mandarin). And to confuse things even further, the Cantonese-speaking Puntis spoke different versions of the Cantonese dialect. For example, the Puntis who lived in the three districts that made up the city of Canton and its immediate suburbs considered their way of speaking Cantonese "purer" than the Cantonese spoken by other Puntis.

If Puntis and Hakkas disliked each other intensely, they had even less use for a third group, the *Tanka*, or "boat people." Many of these Tanka people were born and lived their entire lives on river sampans and sea-going junks. They made their living as fishermen and ferrymen (and sometimes in such related, though illegal, occupations as piracy and smuggling). Tankas were considered such outcasts that they were not even allowed to intermarry with the other people of Kwangtung.

In theory, the Imperial government of China ruled over Kwangtung. But the Emperor and his Court were far, far away in their capital at Peking in North China. Government officials on the Kwangtung scene rarely exerted much control over local affairs. Furthermore,

China's defeat in the Opium War had badly shattered the prestige of the ruling Imperial family. Rebellions broke out in many parts of China. And the warring rebel groups and secret societies added to the general confusion.

The life of the Chinese peasant farmer, in Kwangtung and elsewhere, was not an easy one at any time. In times of stress, his life grew steadily worse. His whole world might have come completely unglued had it not been for the intense loyalty and devotion he had for his own family. This loyalty was especially strong in Chinese rural society.

When a Chinese spoke of his family, he was not referring just to the immediate family of father, mother, brothers and sisters, and maybe grandparents. Instead, he was ordinarily referring to the larger family or clan (the clan is a number of individual families, all of whom claim descent from common ancestors). The positions and relationships of each member of such a Chinese family had long been defined in great detail by such ancient Chinese wise men as Confucius. Filial piety was one of the most important Confucian teachings. It required the young to honor and obey their elders, as well as to honor their ancestors.

For the individual in Chinese village society, the strong family structure was perhaps the only unchanging element in his otherwise constantly changing world. The family was the main source of social control and social protection. In turn, each member of the family was expected to give to—and, if necessary, to make personal sacrifices for—the betterment of the entire family.

In this kind of social system, a person defined his

purpose in life not so much in terms of his own personal happiness. Rather, his main purpose was directed toward ensuring the survival and well-being of the family as a group.

Wealth among country people is often based on the amount of land owned by the family. Chinese peasant families tended to be large while their land holdings— if they had any at all—tended to be small. Moreover, they had little chance to acquire additional land. Most of them were unschooled and unskilled in anything other than the traditional farming methods passed down from father to son.

But, as we have already noted, regions were developing outside of China during the 1840s and 1850s that were in great need of manual laborers. This circumstance presented many a young Chinese peasant with his big opportunity, and set the pattern for the coolie trade described earlier. In effect, he agreed to go to a foreign land and rent out his ability to perform work to foreign employers.

Strangely, it was his deep feelings for his family that caused him to leave his home and village. It is important to understand that he left home *not* because he wished to escape from an old way of life and search for a new one. It was just the opposite. He went to a new country in an effort to save the old way of life at home. While away from home, he would live as cheaply as possible, sending every extra penny back to China for the family he had left behind. And he had every intention of returning to his native village someday to live out his last years with his family and friends.

Thus, his feeling was that of a "sojourner"—one who was a temporary resident of a foreign land. When he agreed to leave China, he physically removed himself from home and family. But his thoughts, his hopes, his purpose remained firmly rooted in the place of his birth.

How long was a temporary stay abroad? Well, in the sojourner's fondest dreams, he would make a great deal of money quickly and then return home to enjoy the fruits of his great good fortune. More realistically, however, he resigned himself to spending most of his adult working life in a foreign country. If he couldn't return home right away, he hoped at least to go back for visits to his native village. Maybe once every five or ten years he would go home for a reunion with his parents and wife—(if he had one, to acquire a wife if he didn't)—to father children to carry on the family name, or just simply to quiet the pangs of homesickness caused by the loneliness of his life in a foreign land.

If everything worked out as he hoped, he would one day return home to stay, having earned enough wealth to buy a choice piece of land in his native village. Honored and respected by all for his long years of effort and sacrifice on behalf of his family, he would then, presumably, live happily ever after.

Or, at least, that was his dream.

CHAPTER FOUR

LAND OF THE
GOLDEN MOUNTAINS

Late in the 1840s, small numbers of Chinese began arriving in San Francisco. Most of them apparently were not young peasants, however, but merchants who came to set up small businesses of one sort or another. Through hard work and saving, some of them did very well for themselves. They were later able to return to their homeland much wealthier than they had been.

Their stay in California, of course, was during the time of the discovery of gold at Sutter's Mill. And it was believed that they were the ones who carried the exciting news back to China.

The dream of the Golden Mountains had a great effect on the pattern of Chinese emigration. Up to 1850, less than a thousand Chinese had made their way to America. Yet, in 1852 alone, more than eighteen thousand Chinese passed through the Golden Gate.

The transporting of Chinese to America quickly became a highly organized business. Most of the ships that brought the Chinese to California sailed from Hong Kong, the British crown colony and free port, down the east bank of the Pearl River from Canton.

A Chinese laborer headed for California, often carrying all his worldly possessions in a single bamboo basket and a bedroll, would first make his way by river boat to Hong Kong. There, he called upon Chinese passage brokers who arranged his cross-Pacific transportation for him through the credit-ticket system. The price of the voyage varied, but in the 1850s it averaged about fifty dollars. This was already a huge sum of money to a Chinese farm lad, but the actual cost of his trip climbed even higher. A British official in Hong Kong once noted that by the time the ticket brokers got through with the interest on the loan and other expenses, the emigrating Chinese laborers were sometimes two hundred dollars in debt.

Almost all the sailing ships used in bringing Chinese to America were foreign-owned, with American and British ships leading the pack. The luckier Chinese emigrants sailed on fast clipper ships which crossed the Pacific in two months' time or less. But as the cross-Pacific traffic increased, even rotten old hulks were pressed into service. These tired, leaky hulks sometimes took as long as four months to complete the ocean crossing. Later, steam-powered vessels were introduced to the China-California run and cut the average passage time to a little over a month.

Conditions aboard the ships making the Pacific crossing seemed to change with ships and shipmasters. For example, when the passenger vessel *Balmoral* arrived in San Francisco from Whampoa in 1852, the ship's captain was presented with a "magnificent silk banner" bearing the inscription: "Presented to J. B. Robertson by 464 of his Chinese passengers who have experienced much kindness and attention from him during the voyage from Kwangtung to the Golden Hills."

In other instances, the story was not nearly so pleasant. To make the largest amount of passage money from their human cargo, some shipmasters treated the emigrating Chinese laborers more as cargo than as humans. The Chinese were sometimes jammed below deck in holds said to be as dank and filthy as any found aboard the old slave ships that sailed from the African coast. There were occasional reports of fights breaking out between ship's crew and passengers, food spoiling during the long, boring trips, and voyages ending in horrible disasters.

In 1854, during an eighty-day crossing on the *Libertad,* one hundred of the five hundred Chinese passengers aboard died before reaching the Golden Gate. In the same year, 86 out of the 613 Chinese passengers aboard the *Exchange* died. American and British maritime laws passed to prevent these evils were rarely enforced on the China-California run. Besides, unscrupulous shipmasters interested only in profits had devised all kinds of ways to get around the rules.

The arrival of hundreds of seasick Chinese newcomers on the docks of San Francisco was usually a scene of noise and confusion. According to those who witnessed such events, the arriving Chinese came down the gangplanks "wearing all their clothes on their backs, layer on top of layer, and carrying small bundles and blankets." On the docks they were met by customs officials, whose greetings consisted of few spoken words but much searching of the newcomers. This was to make sure that no opium was being smuggled in underneath all those layers of clothing.

Then, the representatives of the Chinese companies that had made the travel arrangements took over. Each of these representatives called out in a different local Chinese dialect and assembled the newcomers into groups according to their home districts in Kwangtung. The immigrants piled their few belongings into waiting carts and then trotted off in file behind the carts to the Chinese quarters of San Francisco. There, they were housed in dormitories while awaiting new arrangements to take them out to the gold country.

Gold had attracted the Chinese to California. And most of them wasted little time in going out and looking for some. Often, they organized into groups, with a headman to serve as leader of the band and to take care of such matters as staking out claims. As a newspaper, the *Daily Alta California*, reported in 1852: "A very large party of Celestials (i.e., Chinese) attracted considerable attention yesterday evening . . . on their way to the southern mines. They numbered about fifty, each one carrying a pole, to which was attached large rolls of matting, mining tools, and provisions. . . . They appeared to be in excellent spirits and in great hopes of success, judging from their appearance."

Things didn't quite work out that well.

Though a kind of rough-hewed democracy existed in the gold mining country in the 1850s and everyone was supposed to have an equal chance to mine the gold, some people—those who did not speak English or had darker skin—were apparently "less equal" than others. The white miners did not consider as their equals the

Gold had attracted the Chinese to California. And most of them wasted little time in going out and looking for some.

Indians, Mexicans, and "Chilenos" (a term then used in California to describe all South Americans, whether or not they happened to have come from Chile). And ranked somewhere below them were the Chinese.

As more and more Chinese came to the towns scattered all over the mining country, bad feelings between Chinese and Americans increased accordingly. Some communities drove out the Chinese newcomers by threatening to horsewhip them or to remove them by force. In most places, the Chinese could mine only in regions long since worked over by others and no longer producing much gold. A Foreign Miners' Tax, originally passed to harass Mexican miners, was later applied almost exclusively against the Chinese.

Yet, sometimes through sheer luck, a few Chinese mining groups took out their goodly share of gold from the land. At other times, wealth was made in stranger ways still.

A story was told of a Chinese mining company headman named Ah Sam who, for twenty-five dollars, bought a dirt-floored log cabin from six American miners. As Ah Sam had suspected, the previous owners of the cabin had been careless and had permitted gold dust to fall all over the dirt floor. He put his crew to work washing the dirt in the cabin—and reportedly realized $3000 worth of gold dust from his original $25 investment.

For most of the Chinese who came to California in search of gold, however, mining was much hard work and little return. By the late 1850s, the California gold rush had pretty much run its course and attention was shifting to neighboring Nevada and its fabulous gold and silver strikes in the famed Comstock Lode. A portion of the Chinese miners no longer wished to stay on this side of the Pacific and went back to China. Of the more than sixty thousand Chinese who came to California in the 1850s, perhaps half of them returned home before ten years had passed.

Among those remaining, many continued to work in the mines. But some had to find other jobs. In a frontier society with very few women, the Chinese found ready employment in lines that were usually thought of as women's work—laundering, sewing, or working as household servants.

The Chinese also found employment in many other fields: as fishermen, freight haulers, wood choppers, farm workers, stonecutters, boot and saddle makers—some twenty-five different occupations in all. Among these, probably the least expected was manufacturing cigars at which about 7500 Chinese earned a living at one time.

California developed with the help of Chinese labor. But the greatest tale of Chinese labor in America awaited the 1860s—when construction began on the first transcontinental railroad across the United States.

CHAPTER FIVE

SHORT CUT TO THE ORIENT

James H. Strobridge, construction superintendent of the Central Pacific Railroad Company, was a man who didn't mince words. When he heard of a plan to recruit Chinese laborers to work on his line, his first word was "No!" The whole idea shocked Strobridge. The Chinese coolies he had seen rarely stood taller than five feet or weighed more than 120 pounds. Railroad construction? Why that was heavy work requiring big six-footers like —well, like Strobridge himself. The small Chinese workers simply couldn't do the job.

"I will not boss Chinese," Strobridge stubbornly insisted. "I will not be responsible for work done on the road by Chinese labor. From what I've seen of them, they're not fit laborers anyway."

Still, the superintendent could offer no other solution to the Central Pacific's labor problem. The CP had taken on the enormous job of building the western section of the first railroad to cross the United States. It needed thousands of construction workers but had attracted only a few.

At a time when men hoped to get rich quick in the gold and silver "diggin's" of the West, the idea of working on a railroad at a going pay rate of about a dollar a day (plus board) just didn't seem especially appealing.

In January 1865, Strobridge had advertised all over California for five thousand laborers, offering "constant and permanent" work on the railroad. There was no stampede of applicants to the CP's employment office.

Those who did sign up were usually interested in a temporary job rather than anything "constant and permanent." For many of them, a short stint on the railroad was a way to pick up a grub stake. The ride to the construction camp at the railhead was a form of free transportation taking them that much closer to the gold and silver mines. Out of every hundred workers hired by the CP, less than ten stayed on the job longer than a week.

Unable to recruit even one-quarter of the number of workers he needed, Strobridge gave in a little and grudgingly agreed to accept a few Chinese laborers —on a trial basis, of course.

And so, one cold spring day in 1865, the first crew of fifty Chinese workers piled out of freight cars and shuffled through the railroad work camp. One look at them and Strobridge was sure that his worst fears were true. The Chinese looked every bit as weak and puny as he had expected. The construction superintendent looked down on the Chinese and assigned them only the simplest jobs around camp.

But there was something about the Chinese that made Strobridge take another look. They seemed to learn quickly. They worked with a tireless, methodical determination. Impressed, Strobridge decided to try them out on railroad grading. By the end of the first week, the Chinese crew had completed the longest and smoothest stretch of grading of any crew on the line.

Strobridge was convinced. The message flashed back to company headquarters: "Send up more coolies."

The Central Pacific in Sacramento searched the California countryside for Chinese laborers, hiring them and sending them up to the railhead in groups of fifty at a time. The railroad's increasing demand for workers soon thinned out the local Chinese labor market. The CP turned to the shipping firms, contracting with them to hire and transport workers directly from China.

In a few months' time, the Central Pacific counted its Chinese workers by the thousands. From the summer of 1865 until the rail line was finished four years later, the Chinese would form the main part of the CP's labor force.

No one had planned it that way. But in a sense, the role that men from China played in the building of our first transcontinental railroad was altogether fitting.

For the idea of rails crossing the North American continent was founded on an old dream of a short cut to the Orient. It was a dream that began long before railroads existed. Indeed, it might be said to have begun with the discovery of the New World by Christopher Columbus.

When Columbus pushed off from Spain in 1492, he left no doubt that he hoped to find the rich spice lands

The Chinese borrowed money to sail to America and paid back these loans through such jobs as working on the railroad.

of the Orient. By sailing long enough toward the west, he was certain that he would wind up in the Far East.

Unfortunately, however, he underestimated the size of the world by the width of one continent—America— and one ocean—the Pacific. To the end of his days Columbus believed that the New World he found was really part of the great Asian land mass.

Other explorers followed Columbus in the search for a shipping route to the East. But they were no more successful in their search than Columbus. Gradually, seafaring men resigned themselves to sailing around the land barrier formed by the American continents to reach the Orient.

Nevertheless men still talked hopefully of finding a river flowing across the North American continent and emptying into the Pacific—a "Northwest Passage" to the fabled Orient.

But if some people saw the New World as an obstacle in their path to the Orient, others saw it as a prize. European settlers crossed the Atlantic to settle on the land. They built new towns and cities, and, in time, a new nation on these American shores. It was a nation whose frontier pushed step-by-step westward into the wilderness, first across the Allegheny Mountains and then to the banks of the Mississippi River. In 1803 the administration of President Thomas Jefferson made an agreement with the Emperor Napoleon of France to purchase all French-controlled lands west of the Mississippi. With this agreement, the Louisiana Purchase, United States territory butted up against the Rocky Mountains.

The vision of a nation eventually stretching from one

coast to the other brought back the old dream of an easy route to the Orient. Such a passage, some thought, would assure the role of the young United States in world-wide trade. If no natural trade route existed, men might build one of their own.

In 1818 a St. Louis newspaper editor named Thomas Hart Benton urged the building of a road through the Rockies to link the Missouri River system with the Snake and Columbia rivers of the Pacific Northwest. This river-canal-road link, Benton predicted, would become a new line of communication with eastern Asia and a "channel for the rich commerce which . . . has created so much wealth and power wherever it has flowed."

Meanwhile, new inventions began to reshape the route-to-the-Orient vision.

The age of steam had arrived. In the early 1800s, inventive men in both England and the United States were applying steam power to land transport: a fire-belching "iron horse" that ran on rails. The first steam "locomotivators" frightened as many people as they impressed. The early ones had a tendency to blow up. Nevertheless, a network of rail lines began to fan out over the eastern United States.

Could railroads have a place in the dream of a new trade route to Asia? Among the first to recognize this possibility was Asa Whitney, a Connecticut-born merchant and shipowner who had made a small fortune in the China trade. Whitney reasoned that faster, more direct routes for the Orient trade held out a promise of even bigger fortunes to be made.

In 1845 he decided to stake all he had on the promotion of a transcontinental railroad line. With such a railroad, Whitney pointed out, the United States would be in a strong position to dominate the world trade and transport of the "spices, teas, precious woods, and fabrics of Cathay [China]." He saw a day when practically all the trade between Europe and the Orient would pass through the United States.

"You will see, too," Whitney told his listeners, "that it will change the entire world."

Where should this railroad be built? People held different views on the best route for the cross-continental railroad. Newspaperman Thomas Hart Benton (who by this time had become an important Senator from Missouri) insisted that his own home town St. Louis would be a splendid place to start the project. Baltimore, Charleston, Savannah, Memphis, and New Orleans were among the many other cities mentioned as the possible eastern end of the transcontinental rail line.

Congress studied the proposals, talked and debated, but came to no decision. Northern senators and representatives held out for northern routes. Southern senators and representatives stood firm in favor of southern routes.

Rivalries and arguments among the different sections of the country made it impossible for Congress to decide on a route, and Asa Whitney became its main casualty. His hopes for building a cross-continental railroad gone, Whitney faded out of the picture—broke, disheartened, and soon forgotten by almost everyone.

But the idea of a railroad to the Pacific was not forgotten. For the eyes of America were now firmly fixed westward.

Before 1840 the Yankee presence on the Pacific coast amounted to hardly more than a scattering of fur trappers and occasional visits by ships hailing from New England ports. The spectacularly beautiful Oregon Country (today, the states of Oregon, Washington, Idaho, and the Canadian province of British Columbia) was at that time under the joint control of Britain and the United States. California was still a half-sleepy province of Mexico.

But the 1840s brought a new "westering" surge. The annexation of Texas by the United States led to war with Mexico. The peace treaty forced Mexico to cede all of its land north of the Rio Grande, including California, to the United States. Then in 1848 the boundary line between U.S. and British territories in the Pacific Northwest was settled by mutual agreement.

American pioneers began to wend their way westward in growing numbers. Along the Mormon Trail, the Oregon Trail, and the California Trail came explorers and trappers, to be followed by miners, farmers, merchants and homesteaders. With the discovery of gold in California in 1848, the trickle of migrants turned into a stream and then a torrent.

The pioneers who went west were a sturdy bunch. They had to be. For them, just getting there was an ordeal of heroic proportions.

For westering homesteaders, their mule- or oxen-drawn wagons piled high with all their belongings, the overland route meant month after month of patient plodding across broad prairies, dry deserts, and through mountain passes. They suffered from thirst in the dry country. They shivered in the freezing cold of the high country. They fought off attacks by Indians whose land they were crossing.

Commercial stagecoach lines later cut the traveling time by a great deal. An express coach could make the run from St. Louis to San Francisco in about a month's time—provided the passengers did not mind traveling day and night and were not too particular about frequent rest stops.

If the traveler did not want to go by land he could go by sea. Ships, powered by sail or steam or both, regularly sailed from the East coast to the West coast and back by way of the long-established Cape Horn route. But this meant a voyage of more than eight thousand miles down the Atlantic coast of the American continents, around storm-lashed Cape Horn at the tip of South America, and then back some seven thousand more miles up the Pacific coast to California. With luck, the voyage could be completed in four months, however, six to eight months sailing along this route was not unusual.

'Round Cape Horn remained for many years a main route for heavy freight, but most seagoing passengers chose a shorter route that took advantage of Central American geography. Following this route, passengers boarded steamers at East coast ports for the trip to Chagres on the Caribbean coast of Panama. There, they left ship and marched overland twenty-four miles along a jungle trail across the narrow Panamanian isthmus. Arriving at Panama City on the Pacific side, they boarded another ship for the rest of their journey to San Francisco. Still, the Panama route was very risky: travelers were often exposed to tropical diseases while waiting around the fever-ridden isthmus for travel connections.

No matter which route was chosen, the journey west was always long, boring, and often dangerous. As a folk saying of the time expressed it: "The cowards never started and the weak died along the way." The wonder of it all was that so many managed, somehow, to arrive at the end of their journey with their hopes and health intact. When California entered the Union in 1850 as our thirty-first state, it counted nearly one hundred thousand residents. Just three years after that, the population of our first Pacific coast state had tripled.

This rapid growth in the West presented the United States with a curious new national problem. The nation was growing up in two separated sections on opposite sides of a continent. In between lay some two thousand miles of almost empty land. Unless the distance between the American East and the American West was joined by faster means of transportation and communication, the East and West were in danger of losing touch with each other. They might develop not as a single nation but as two. America's westward destiny added one more very strong reason for building a transcontinental railroad.

The Pacific railroad, however, would remain mostly talk—until the outbreak of the American Civil War in 1861.

Now, the nation was in very serious trouble. The

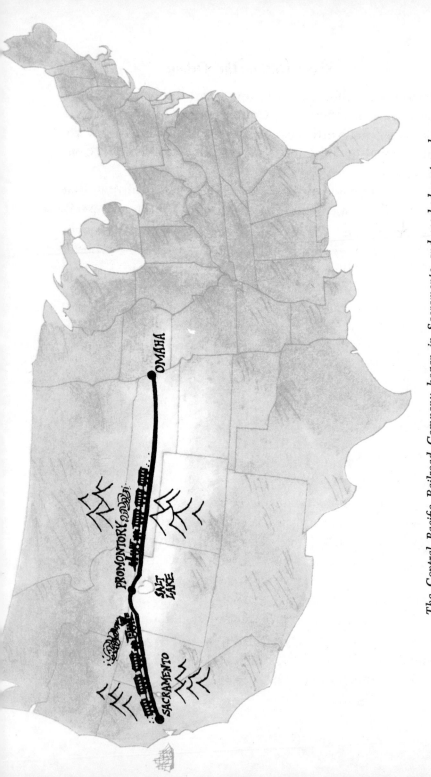

The Central Pacific Railroad Company began in Sacramento and worked eastward, and the Union Pacific started near Omaha and built westward.

Union was in danger of falling apart as Southern states withdrew to form the Confederacy. In the struggle between the North and the South, would the West remain loyal to the Union? Or would it choose the Confederacy?

The leaders of Congress (what was left of it now that its Southern members had packed up and gone home) pressed for the immediate construction of a transcontinental railroad. By linking the West to the North, they argued, Western loyalty to the Union could be counted upon.

So it was that a Pacific Railway Bill made a fast passage through the two houses of Congress. On July 1, 1862, President Abraham Lincoln signed it into law.

This Pacific Railway Act chartered two railroad construction companies to build and operate the cross-continental line. The Central Pacific Railroad Company would begin construction in California, at Sacramento, and work eastward. A second company, the Union Pacific, would start near Omaha, Nebraska, and build westward until its line met the CP's. As originally planned, the two rail lines were supposed to meet somewhere near the California-Nevada border.

To help pay for this gigantic undertaking, the Pacific Railway Act of 1862 provided government help to the railroad companies. The companies would receive grants of free land along the railroad right of way. More immediately important, the federal government promised cash loans: $16,000 for each mile of construction in low-lying areas; $32,000 for each mile of rail line laid in the deserts and high plateaus, and $48,000 per mile where the going would be toughest—in the mountains.

CHAPTER SIX

TOILING ON THE
LONG IRON TRAIL

At last the work could begin. On January 8, 1863, officials of the Central Pacific Railroad Company, joined by a large number of Sacramento's population, broke ground to mark the start of the great iron trail in the West.

That must have been a proud moment for Theodore Dehone Judah, a brilliant young civil engineer who had, almost singlehandedly, brought the CP into being. It was he who had found and surveyed a possible route for a continent-crossing railroad through California's towering Sierra Nevada mountains. And it was he who, for years, had mounted an almost one-man campaign for the Pacific railroad venture.

Judah had had to put up with the insults of name-callers—"Crazy Judah," they called him. But he had refused to be put off. Eventually he won the support of a group of Californian businessmen, headed by four very successful Sacramento storekeepers: Collis P. Huntington and Mark Hopkins, partners in a hardware store; Leland Stanford, a wholesale grocer who had political ambitions; and Charles Crocker, a dry goods merchant.

Though the backgrounds of the four Sacramento storekeepers hardly suggested railroad millionaires in the making, they were all able, successful, and ambitious men. After Theodore Judah's death in 1863, they took control of the Central Pacific and guided it to completion. In time they would gain fame (and a fortune apiece) as the "Big Four Associates" of Pacific railroading.

The members of the Big Four pooled their talents and became a smoothly operating group. The CP elected Leland Stanford president. A good choice, it appeared, since he had also been elected governor of California. In his two roles, Stanford was in a fine position to promote plenty of good will and sympathy between the state government and the railroad company.

The title of CP vice-president went to Collis Huntington, a man with a well-founded reputation as a shrewd, wise trader. During the building of the CP, Huntington would spend most of his time on the East coast. Here he acted as the CP's combination fund raiser, purchasing agent, and contact with Congress.

Mark Hopkins (not to be confused with a famous New England educator of the same name who lived at about the same time) was a sober, sad-faced man who shied away from public attention. His caution and restraint made him a natural choice as treasurer and keeper of the CP's financial records.

To big, cheerful Charles Crocker—"Charlie" to one and all—went the job of directing the actual construction work on the Central Pacific. He was said to be full of energy and surprisingly light-footed for a man weighing more than 240 pounds. At one time or another

Crocker had worked at a half-dozen different jobs, from farming to foundry work to storekeeping. True, he had never built a railroad. But his lack of railroading experience bothered him not at all. "I know," Crocker explained with his usual confidence, "how to manage men."

Despite their outward self-assurance, the builders of the Central Pacific knew that they faced huge problems. There was little money in the CP's treasury. Except for a large supply of locally grown timber (for railroad ties, bridges, and trestles), practically all the other supplies and heavy equipment had to be ordered from factories in the East. Ships sailing around Cape Horn to California carried the materials.

The CP's shopping list included everything from rolling stock (locomotives and cars) to wrought iron rails (weighing fifty-six pounds to the yard) to spikes, "fishplates" (used to connect one rail to another), and hundreds and hundreds of kegs of blasting powder.

Since the Civil War was raging at the time, hardware was not easy to come by. Huntington had to use all his skill and cleverness to keep the supplies flowing toward California. Even so, wartime prices and shipping expenses increased the cost of everything. The price of blasting powder rose from $2.50 to $15.00 a keg. Iron rails which could be bought for $55 a ton in 1861 climbed to a peak price of $262 a ton at one point during the Civil War.

The CP's first order of rails didn't arrive in California until a full nine months after the ground breaking ceremony in January. On October 26, 1863, its first rail was spiked down on Sacramento's Front Street. Three weeks after that, the CP's first locomotive, nicknamed the *Governor Stanford,* puffed along a few hundred yards of track. Its shrieking whistle announced to all that the CP had indeed begun to roll.

Though Charlie Crocker later admitted that he had to learn how to build a railroad as he went along, Crocker's construction crews gradually pushed the tracks eastward. By April 1864, Sacramento and the town of Roseville were connected by eighteen miles of track. Soon, the CP had enough rolling stock to begin regular passenger service—service regular enough to warrant the publishing of a timetable.

Crocker moved up and down the track, in his own words, "bellowing like a bull" to urge his work crews on to greater efforts. But as the trackage became longer, he found that he couldn't be everywhere at once. Thereupon, he hired James Harvey Strobridge to take command of the work crews at the end of the track. A tall, angular, fierce-looking man, Strobridge had a terrible temper and a choice collection of cuss words. When men worked for Strobridge, they worked hard—just out of sheer fright.

Even with Crocker bellowing and Strobridge cussing, the construction pace was not fast enough. Government money flowed into the CP's treasury only as fast as each mile of track could be put down. At the rate the CP was moving forward, it was in no danger of becoming rich.

Railroad builders in those days did not have steam shovels, or bulldozers, or power drills. All they had were hand tools—picks and shovels, crowbars, axes, and sledge hammers—and blasting powder. Mounds of dirt and rocks were hauled by wheelbarrows and one-horse dump carts. Most of all, railroad construction depended on the muscles and sweat of men.

The Central Pacific needed an army of workmen. But it could barely muster a regiment-sized working force. The glitter of silver and gold in Nevada's Comstock Lode across the mountains lured away hundreds of workers. They all dreamed of fast fortunes and high living in boom towns such as Virginia City and Carson City.

By 1865 the CP's labor problems became so serious that its directors even played with the idea of asking the U.S. government to send Confederate prisoners of war out west to work on the railroad. But the idea was never carried out for the Civil War ended in that year.

At this point, Charlie Crocker came up with an answer to the CP's labor shortage. Over the objections of Strobridge, Crocker issued an order to his construction superintendent: "Hire the Chinese."

Within six months after the first group of Chinese arrived in the CP's work camp, they had been joined by two thousand more of their countrymen. Each work train arriving at the railhead brought more of the blue-shirted, basket-hatted Oriental workmen to the construction site.

The reinforcement from the Orient was arriving at a critical time. By now the CP's railhead was at Clipper Gap, forty-three miles out of Sacramento. Graders building the roadbed ahead of the track-laying crews were climbing up the ridges into the high country. The work grew more difficult with each passing mile. For the CP had come face to face with a solid wall of granite—a mountain range called the Sierra Nevada.

The Sierra Nevada range was well named. Translated into English, the words mean "snow-capped saw." The Sierra Nevada is just that—a range of saw-toothed peaks and ridges jutting up suddenly from the valley floor. Most winters, the mountain passes there became clogged with tons and tons of snow, a death trap for those caught or lost in it.

On the route of the CP, the high Sierras crested at more than seven thousand feet above sea level. But there was no way to get around it. The CP had to go over and through the mountains. It meant tunneling and bridging on a scale never before tried.

Directed by Crocker and Strobridge, the Chinese workmen began a massed human assault against the mountains. The hillsides rang with the sound of a thousand picks and drills pecking away. The mountains echoed with constant thunder of exploding gunpowder. Inch by inch, the workmen gouged and carved a path for the railroad up the steep cliffs.

To Albert D. Richardson, a New York *Tribune* reporter visiting the CP construction site, the Chinese formed "a great army laying siege to nature in her strongest citadel." Wrote Richardson: "The rugged mountains looked like stupendous anthills. They swarmed with Celestials (Chinese), shoveling, wheeling, carting, drilling, and blasting rock and earth."

Along some stretches, the cliffsides provided no footholds at all—not even for mountain goats. The Chinese found a clever way to overcome this problem.

"*The rugged mountains looked like stupendous anthills. They swarmed with Celestials (Chinese), shoveling, wheeling, carting, drilling, and blasting rock and earth.*"

With reeds sent up from San Francisco, the Chinese wove big round wicker baskets with sides about waist-high. The baskets were then hauled up to the top of the mountain. There, one or two Chinese workmen climbed into each basket, and the rig—men and basket—was lowered by rope and pulley over the side of the cliff.

Dangling dangerously in their baskets thousands of feet above the valley floor, the Chinese workmen chipped a series of holes in the cliffside, stuffing each hole with blasting powder. The fuse was lit, a hand signal given, and the baskets were quickly hauled up in a frantic scramble to safety. The explosion that followed announced that a few more feet of ledge had been blasted out of the mountainside.

Sometimes the baskets were not hauled up fast enough. Sometimes the ropes snapped, and men and baskets tumbled thousands of feet down the cliffside. The number of Chinese who fell to their deaths in the high Sierras will never be known. The CP kept no records of casualties among its work force. But these were only the first of an estimated five hundred to one thousand Chinese workmen who were to lose their lives before the mountains were finally conquered.

The courage of the Chinese workmen in the mountains proved a real eye opener to the other men working for the CP.

When the Chinese first arrived on the scene, the white workers had greeted them with howling laughter and catcalls. Some of the whites swore that they would not work within a hundred yards of a "heathen Chinese." Others grumbled that the willingness of the Chinese to work for less pay held down their own wage scale.

But Crocker met these grumblings head on. The CP had to hire the Chinese, he explained, because it couldn't get nearly enough white workers to do the job. And if the whites couldn't learn to get along with the Chinese —well, then, the CP would have to let the white workers go and hire only the Chinese. Crocker's threat hit its mark. The grumbling ended.

In any event, the white workers soon discovered that their Oriental companions proved inoffensive. They kept to themselves. They bothered no one. Moreover, they freed the white workers from the drudgery of the pick and shovel. Many of the whites found themselves promoted to foremen and crew chiefs to supervise the work of the Chinese crews. With the increase in pay and self-respect of the white workers, labor peace prevailed on the CP.

The Chinese workmen were themselves organized into crews numbering twelve to twenty members. Each crew worked and lived together as a unit. They lived in tents or huts. They slept on simple wooden cots.

Each crew was led by a Chinese headman who kept discipline among his men. On pay days, the headman collected the wages for his entire crew, later distributing the money to each member. Most of the headmen could speak just enough English to do a little translating. But language rarely proved a problem. The Chinese workers learned quickly through watching others. Once shown how to do a job, they were fast to figure out the rest of it by themselves.

Each crew also hired its own Chinese cook. Imported Chinese groceries were sent up the line periodically by merchants in San Francisco. Each member of the crew shared in the cost of his food. For the Chinese workers, the main diet included dried oysters, abalone, bamboo shoots and bean sprouts, crackers and noodles, Chinese bacon, pork and poultry. To the CP's white workers, surviving on a diet of boiled beef, bread, potatoes, and coffee, the menus of the Chinese crews were a source of endless wonderment.

In addition, the Chinese drank tea by the gallons. Even while they worked, "tea boys" trotted up to the Chinese work gangs dispensing hot tea, transported in old whiskey barrels suspended from the ends of a long pole. Tea drinking, especially out where the quality of the drinking water was none too certain, had its advantages. Tea requires the water to be boiled, thus assuring that the water was safe for drinking. Besides, no one has ever been known to get drunk on tea, and the Chinese workers never suffered from morning-after hangovers.

One other thing about the Chinese amazed their fellow workers on the CP. Before supper each night, the members of the Chinese work crews lined up before barrels filled with warm water. Then, one after another, they stripped off their dirty clothing, bathed themselves, and changed into clean clothes. Out in the rough and rugged West during those frontier days, such personal cleanliness was considered somewhat unusual.

Indeed, to the casual observer, the Chinese work crews appeared to be disciplined, smooth-working human machines. They worked from dawn to dusk with few breaks and fewer complaints. They hardly ever seemed to get sick, or even tired.

Those who watched more carefully, however, knew that this wasn't quite so. One of these, a Swiss student named Hemmann Hoffmann who worked for a while on the CP, noted that each Chinese crew kept a few spare workers available. When one of the regular workers became ill—or if he just didn't feel like working on a particular day—a substitute would take his place. This made the Chinese able to report with a full work crew each morning.

Yet, the hard work and endurance of the Chinese working for the CP needed no apologies. As Charles Crocker wrote of his Chinese crews: "Wherever we put them, we found them good, and they worked themselves into our favor to such an extent that if we found we were in a hurry for a job of work, it was better to put Chinese on at once."

Little wonder that from this time on, the CP's Chinese workers were called "Crocker's Pets."

CHAPTER SEVEN

CROCKER'S PETS

In 1866 the CP's Chinese work force swelled to ten thousand strong. "Crocker's Pets" seemed to be swarming all over the high Sierras, doing whatever the CP wanted done.

They toppled the tall trees and rooted out the stumps. They broke and carted rock. They graded the climbing roadbed, put down the ties, and spiked home the rails. But the hardest job of all was tunneling.

The Sierra crossing called for a dozen tunnels before the tracks reached the Nevada border (and three more after that). The tunnels were of different lengths. Seven of them clustered within two miles of the place where the CP's cross-mountain route climbed to its highest point. The longest one, called the Summit Tunnel, meant drilling 1659 feet through solid granite.

The CP's engineers figured that it might take as long as a year and a half to bore through the Summit Tunnel. They put five hundred Chinese on the job at once, organizing them into three eight-hour shifts working around the clock. The Chinese worked at both ends of the tunnel at the same time, digging toward the middle. Later, a shaft was sunk down to the center of the tunnel, and work crews lowered into the hole to dig from the inside out as well.

Still, progress was agonizingly slow. The rock proved so hard that black powder simply blew out of the drill holes without shattering the rock face. Despite the unending labor of the Chinese workers, progress through the rock was measured at only seven or eight inches a day!

As the year 1866 wore on, weather became more and more of a problem. The rains came down in torrents, causing washouts, turning roads into mud baths, and fouling up the CP's supply system.

In colder, higher ground, the dampness from the skies came down as snow, snow, and more snow. The Sierra was living up to its name. From November until the following May, the clouds would dump some forty-five feet of snow on the mountain.

Soon even the snowplows could not get through the clogged mountain passes. Work along the rail line came to a standstill. Crocker was forced to send the main part of his work force back down from the mountains. But he kept several hundred of his strongest Chinese laborers up in the cliffs to work on the tunnels all through the wintry months.

Wind-whipped snowdrifts soon buried the camps, entirely covering the huts of the workmen. They had to bore through the packed snow for air shafts to the surface. To get to and back from work, they had to carve out a maze of snow tunnels, some of them two hundred feet long.

Through the terrible winter, the Chinese workers burrowed under the piles of snow almost like human moles. They lived through the bitter cold, never seeing sunshine or the open sky. Often the food supply ran short, and the men survived on daily doses of cornmeal and tea.

Now, as the snow piled higher and higher, a new danger arose: avalanche! Tons of snow came sliding down from the higher cliffs, sweeping and burying all before it. Snow tunnels caved in. Men just disappeared beneath the roaring, tumbling snow slides. Their frozen bodies would not be found until the snow began to melt in the thaw of the following spring. Some of them would be found still tightly clutching picks and shovels in their lifeless hands.

But spring came at last. And Crocker threw his army of Chinese laborers into a renewed assault against the Sierras. Normally, the work went on six days a week, pausing only on Sunday. Sometimes, it didn't even stop on Sundays.

Finally, on August 29, 1867, came cause for rejoicing. The men boring the tunnel at the summit broke through. The Summit Tunnel was quickly finished off. By November 30 the men had completed laying track through this granite cavern.

As the year 1867 ended, the builders of the Central Pacific could at last enjoy a measure of pride. The CP had laid down about 130 miles of track from Sacramento across the mountains. Except for a seven-mile gap and some smaller tunnels to be finished later, the CP had crossed the high Sierras and reached the Nevada border.

The men who challenged the mountains had won.

When the Pacific Railway Act was first passed in 1862, most observers had expected the Central Pacific and the Union Pacific to link up somewhere in the area of the California-Nevada line. They thought that the Sierra crossing was about as much as the CP would be able to finish before it bumped into the UP's tracks streaking westward from Nebraska.

In 1866, however, Collis Huntington went to work in Washington, D.C., to get Congress to change the ground rules. He was very convincing. Congress changed the Railway Act to allow each company to continue laying tracks until the two lines met—wherever that might be.

Under these rules, the Central Pacific and the Union Pacific no longer looked upon each other as partners in the transcontinental railroad. They now considered each other as competitors.

Every mile of track that each company put down meant more government money flowing into the company's treasury (and that much less money flowing into the other company's treasury). Each mile meant more free land for the railroads—land that could later be sold to the public at a huge profit. And the mileage that each company completed would determine how much of the transcontinental line each would control when the long, long railroad was finished.

At the start of 1868, the Union Pacific seemed to be having much the better of the competition. Its tracks reached out more than five hundred miles from its starting point near Omaha. The UP had really picked up speed after 1866, when two ex-Union generals took charge. General Grenville M. Dodge became the UP's chief engineer while General John Casement (aided by his peppery younger brother Daniel) directed the UP's construction crews. Jack Casement's men fought off Indian attacks and outlaw raiders, braved bitterly cold temperatures—and still set new track-laying records as they went along.

Against the UP record, the Central Pacific had less than 140 miles of track out of Sacramento. But Charles Crocker was not about to give in. He knew that the UP's tracks crossed the Midwest plains, easy work compared to the land that the CP had just come through. Only now was the UP beginning to battle the mountains in Wyoming. The Union Pacific's men would soon find out what railroading through the mountains was all about.

For the Central Pacific, on the other hand, the most difficult stretch was now nearly completed. Ahead were the high tablelands of northern Nevada—dry, lonely, but more or less flat. After the CP's experience in the Sierra Nevada, a little flatness was something to be thankful for.

Charlie Crocker confidently predicted that his crews would average a mile of track for every working day in 1868. The race was on between the CP and the UP.

The Central Pacific now had a labor force numbering some fourteen thousand, about twelve thousand of them Chinese. Most of them by now were veteran railroaders toughened by the rigors of the Sierra crossing. Their numbers impressed Charlie Crocker greatly. He cheerfully laid claim to the honor of commanding the largest single civilian labor force in existence in the world—and, at that time, he was very probably right.

Day after day, a well-drilled routine repeated itself at the CP's advanced construction camps. A shrieking locomotive whistle at dawn announced the start of the workday. The workers stumbled out of their tents and hitched up the horses and mules to the wagons for the ride to the railhead. Along the way, they picked up the rails, ties, and other supplies dumped along the sides of the track by supply trains during the night. They worked all day, extending the ribbon of iron rails into the Nevada desert—until another shriek of the locomotive whistle announced quitting time at dusk.

Week after week, the procession moved eastward. Far out ahead, the surveying teams marked out the route for the track. Then came the grading crew preparing the roadbed. Following them were the track crews. And keeping pace with the track layers were the telegraph crews, setting up poles and stringing wire along the rail route. At the end of each day, a daily progress report was flashed by telegraph down the line to Sacramento.

Month after month, the miles ticked by. Along the railroad's course, new towns sprang up almost overnight: Reno, Wadsworth, Winnemucca, Golconda.

The routine, repeated over and over again, was boring. But it produced wonders. By the end of the year 1868, the Central Pacific's tracks reached Elko, three-quarters of the way across Nevada. The CP's work crews had made good Crocker's boast. In a year's time, they had completed more than 350 miles of track!

But as the two railroads sprinted into Utah, strange things were beginning to happen. CP and UP surveying teams passed each other going in opposite directions. It became obvious that the Union Pacific planned to continue westward until its own tracks reached the

Pacific coast. And the Central Pacific, likewise, would keep going eastward until somebody stopped it, somewhere.

By the spring of 1869, both the Central Pacific's grading crews (made up mostly of Chinese) and the Union Pacific's graders (made up mostly of Irishmen) were working in Utah. Often they built roadbeds that ran side by side, sometimes only one hundred feet or so apart.

The men of the rival railroads looked at each other—and apparently didn't like what they saw. Irishmen battled Chinese with fists and pick handles. Both sides set off explosive charges along their gradings—without bothering to warn the men on the other side—causing many serious injuries. The feud almost got completely out of hand. But, finally, the two crews agreed to a tense truce.

From far away in Washington, D.C., Congress also ordered the two railroads to cut out the foolishness. The lawmakers picked out a spot in Utah, just north of the Great Salt Lake, as the place where the tracks of the two railroads would join. It was a place called Promontory.

Before the tracks of the Central Pacific and the Union Pacific met, however, one bit of high drama remained to be played out.

Crocker had long been annoyed by Union Pacific claims for laying the most trackage in a single day. The UP's record stood at a fraction over eight miles, even though the UP's track crews actually had to put in a twenty-hour workday to accomplish this feat. "They bragged about it," Crocker later recalled, "and it was heralded all over the country as being the biggest day's track laying that ever was known."

The CP's construction boss was sure that his Chinese workers could do better. He and Strobridge assembled a hand-picked crew of 848 men, forty-one teams of horses and carts, and five train loads of supplies and equipment. By April 28, 1869, all was in readiness. Crocker even invited a delegation from the Union Pacific to come over and watch the show.

At seven in the morning, a locomotive whistle signaled the start of the contest. Chinese workers swarmed aboard the first supply train and began to pitch rails, spikes, and bolts off the cars. The first sixteen-car supply train was unloaded in eight minutes flat! It was then rolled back to a siding, and another supply train took its place.

At the same time, other Chinese gangs loaded the equipment aboard small flatcars and rolled the goods up to the rail end. There, eight burly Irish iron handlers awaited them. Working in two four-man teams, the Irishmen heaved 120 feet of rail a minute off the carts (each rail was thirty feet long and weighed 560 pounds!). They raced to keep up with the crew ahead of them setting and aligning the ties.

Behind the iron handlers came still another crew, spiking the rails to the ties and bolting the rail connectors. And behind them came the biggest crew of all, four hundred "gandy dancers" waddling along to tamp down the roadbed.

The entire procession stretched out for nearly two miles. Yet, it moved with awesome precision. An army

At seven in the morning a locomotive whistle signaled the start of the contest. By 7:00 p.m., Crocker's Pets were the new world's track-laying champions.

officer said watching the scene: "I never saw such organization as that. It was just like an army marching over the ground and leaving the track built behind it."

By the time Strobridge called a short lunch halt at 1:30 in the afternoon, the Central Pacific had six miles of new track shimmering in the Utah flats.

Work started up again after lunch. But now the track began to curve and the work went more slowly as the rails had to be bent. Even so, at the final whistle shortly after 7 P.M., Crockers Pets were the new world's track-laying champions. They had put down more than ten miles of track in twelve hours, set 25,800 ties, heaved 3520 lengths of rails, driven more than 55,000 spikes, attached 14,080 bolts and 7040 rail-connecting plates. The eight Irish iron handlers together lifted 1000 tons— 2,000,000 pounds—of rail and could be excused for feeling a bit worn out by day's end.

Crocker had his record. There was hardly anything left to do for an encore—except to link-up with the Union Pacific.

The "Last Rail" ceremonies were scheduled to take place on May 8, 1869. Officers of the Central Pacific who could not make it out to Promontory arranged for elaborate ceremonies to be held at the same time in California.

But complications set in, and the Promontory ceremonies had to be put off a day or two. It was too late to change the plans of the Californians. So they went ahead and began their celebrations as planned on May 8—two days before the rest of the country.

In Sacramento, it was a time for marching bands, parades, cheers, backslapping, and speechmaking. In a proud speech, Crocker praised his "Pets."

"In the midst of our rejoicing, I wish to call to mind that the early completion of this railroad we have built has been in a great measure due to that poor, destitute class of laborers called the Chinese—to the fidelity and industry they have shown—and the great amount of laborers of this land that have been employed upon this work."

His was the only speech which told of the contributions of Chinese labor in the building of the transcontinental rail link.

Two days later, on May 10, six and a half years of determined effort were reaching a climax at Promontory, Utah. A Central Pacific locomotive, the *Jupiter,* and a Union Pacific locomotive, *No. 119,* sat almost headlamp to headlamp. Behind the *Jupiter,* the Central Pacific tracks stretched 690 miles back to Sacramento. Behind the *119,* the Union Pacific tracks stretched 1086 miles toward Omaha. Between the two locomotives, a gap of one-rail length remained.

CP President Leland Stanford came to Promontory well equipped with expensive hardware. He brought two gold spikes from California, a gold and silver spike (the gift of Nevada), and a gold, silver, and iron spike (the gift of Arizona). To drive home the last spikes, Stanford had a silver-plated sledge hammer. The final tie, made especially for the occasion, was of polished California laurel, with a silver plate suitably inscribed. (All this expensive material, of course, could hardly be left to weather and rot under railroad tracks. It was promptly

On May 10, 1869, the Central Pacific and Union Pacific joined to finish the transcontinental railroad. Bret Harte wrote of the event: "Facing on a single track, half a world behind each back."

removed for safekeeping after the ceremonies and less expensive hardware put in its place.

The Golden Spike ceremonies officially got under way shortly after high noon. James Strobridge and his counterpart on the UP, Samuel Reed, set the laurel tie in place. A team of Irish trackmen hefted the last rail into place for the Union Pacific, while a crew of Chinese did the same for the Central Pacific. The honor of tapping in the golden spikes was shared by Stanford and Dr. Thomas C. Durant, vice-president of the UP.

At about 12:40 P.M., the railroad was finished. The message was flashed along the telegraph wires. In cities from coast to coast, fire whistles shrieked, church bells pealed, and cannons boomed out a roaring salute.

The dream of a new route to the Orient—the dream which first spurred the idea of a transcontinental rail-road—did not come true. For only a few months after the Union Pacific and Central Pacific met at Promontory, another great engineering marvel was completed half-way around the world. That was the Suez Canal, a man-made waterway through Egypt connecting the Mediter-ranean Sea and the Red Sea. The Suez Canal, not the U.S. transcontinental railroad, would draw the main part of the commercial traffic between Europe and the Far East.

But the transcontinental railroad had a great effect on the future of the United States as a nation. With the first transcontinental rail line, it became possible to move people and goods from one coast to the other in five days' traveling time. No longer was the American

West cut off from the American East. In helping to break down the problem of distance, the first transcontinental railroad opened the West to rapid development. In turn, the strength and wealth of the growing American nation was greatly helped by the riches of the West.

Perhaps the Chinese laborers—the thousands who crossed an ocean to work in a strange land far from their homes—never fully understood what a continent-spanning railroad was all about. Yet, their courage, their hard work, and their endurance had helped to turn the dream of a long iron trail into reality.

CHAPTER EIGHT

DOUBLE TROUBLE

Almost from the start, Californians tended to look upon the arriving Chinese immigrants with puzzled interest. The Chinese language sounded strange to Californian ears. The Chinese were not Christians and followed different customs. And—well, the Chinese just did not look like any other groups of people on the California scene.

It was not simply that the Chinese had skin that was a shade darker than the whites'. Most of them, for example, dressed differently from other Californians. A few of the Chinese apparently began wearing the red flannel shirts which seemed to be so popular out in the mining country. Some even bought fedora hats for in-town wear. In the mining and railroad work camps, most of the Chinese laborers exchanged their cloth slippers for Western-style boots.

But by and large the Chinese continued to dress as they had back in their villages before coming to the Golden Mountains. They wore loose-fitting, dark blue cotton blouses and baggy trousers to match, a way of dressing that in a later time would invariably be described as pajama-like.

To Californians, Chinese hair styles seemed the strangest of all. In those days, male Chinese shaved their foreheads. They let the hair on the back of their heads grow to great lengths. They then braided it into a single queue (pronounced *kew*) dangling down the back to the waist.

The sight of men wearing their hair in pigtail style left Californians puzzled. Many thought it was some sort of Chinese religious rite. Actually it was a custom begun in the 17th century when a people of northeast Asia conquered China. The conquerors forced all male Chinese to wear a queue as a sign of surrender. By the 19th century, queue-wearing by adult men had become a fully accepted custom in China—so much so that a Chinese man would no more think of cutting off his queue than many American men of those times would think of shaving off their bushy beards.

In any event, the arrival of Chinese in California during those early days caused no alarm. People thought of them as one more colorful group to add to the many different kinds of people that made up early Californian society. San Franciscans, indeed, looked on with civic pride as a Little China—forerunner of San Francisco's famed Chinatown—grew up in their city. The people of Little China were widely thought of as peaceful, law abiding, and hard working people. This was rare in a city which, at that time, was not especially known for its respect for law and order. Moreover, the willingness of the Chinese to join in public events never failed to give an exciting touch to San Francisco's parades and celebrations.

In his annual message to the California legislature in 1852, Governor John McDougal described the Chinese as "one of the most worthy classes of our newly adopted citizens." He asked the state to welcome more Chinese and give them land grants. To the governor, Chinese laborers "who will work faithfully for low wages" would be perfect for work on such projects as turning California's swamplands into good farming land.

Governor McDougal meant well. But his call, among others, to use Chinese laborers touched off a heated argument. Many people worried about the effects of cheap foreign labor on the system of free labor practices in California (free in the sense of free, independent men and not in the sense of work without pay). The argument spread. It marked the beginning of the end of an all too brief period of good will between Californians and Chinese.

The year 1852 saw a sudden spurt in the number of Chinese arriving in California—more than eighteen thousand of them in that year alone. As more Chinese came through the Golden Gate, many Californians began to take a different view of these Asian newcomers. There was increased talk—and fear—of an endless stream of Asian immigrants flooding into the American West.

To a large extent, people's fears were based on money and jobs. What each Californian felt about the Chinese coming to America depended on his own position in the Californian economy. Those with money—rich men like employers and investors—wanted as many Chinese as possible to come to California. California needed many men to work the land. The Chinese seemed to be the one group willing to take on such backbreaking jobs as reclaiming swamplands—work usually shunned by other groups. Those who wanted Chinese laborers pointed out that they worked hard in their own homeland for low pay. Californian businessmen believed that a lot of cheap Asian labor would help the state grow and become richer.

The workingmen of California, however, saw things quite differently. To them these Asian coolies meant unfair competition for jobs. The workingmen felt that the Chinese were a threat to their way of earning a living. They accused Californian businessmen of using Asian laborers to hold down the wages and living standards of all working people. This was an outcry heard over and over again in the years to come.

In 1852, John Bigler took over the state house. And in just about the time it took to change governors, the official attitude toward the Chinese also changed.

The new governor wasted little time in calling on the state legislature to stop further immigration from China. At first, the state lawmakers ignored the governor's request. But from this time on, whenever business was bad and jobs grew scarce in California, the Chinese found themselves singled out as scapegoats for public attack.

Prejudice against the Chinese began and grew in the gold mining regions. There, the Chinese miners were robbed, beaten, cheated, and pushed around by just about every other group of people. Out of the mines and work camps came a well-known saying, "Not a Chinaman's chance." To be a Chinese in California in those times was to have little, if any, chance at all.

A Chinese, back in those days, was not even a second-class citizen. In fact, he was not allowed to be a citizen. This position was later upheld by the state courts and in

The Chinese seemed to be the one group willing to take on such backbreaking jobs as building the railroad and reclaiming the swamplands.

1871 by the U. S. Supreme Court. As a non-citizen, a Chinese in America did not have the right to vote.

Nor did the Chinese find much comfort, let alone protection, in the law. In 1854, the California State Supreme Court ruled that people of color (that is, Asians, Negroes, American Indians, etc.) would not be permitted to testify in court against a white man. As author Samuel Clemens—the famous Mark Twain—noted in his book *Roughing It:* "Any white man can swear a Chinaman's life away in the courts, but no Chinaman can testify against a white man."

Local ordinances and state laws set up special taxes which, in practice, only the Chinese had to pay. The Foreign Miners Licensing Law put a tax of $3 a month on all foreign miners, but it seemed that the only foreign miners that interested the tax collectors were Chinese miners. A similar fishing tax was passed to discourage Chinese fishermen from competing with white fishermen. And for a time there was also a $50 head tax aimed specifically at immigrants who could never become U.S. citizens.

All of these discriminatory tax laws were later repealed or overturned by the courts. But while the laws remained on the books, they helped make the Chinese feel very unwelcome in California. These laws did not stop the Chinese from coming to the Golden Mountains, but they did tend to slow down the numbers of Chinese arriving in California.

The confused Asian newcomers soon became the favorite target of San Francisco's hoodlum gangs. The Reverend Otis Gibson angrily wrote of what the Chinese suffered at the hands of the hoodlums: "They follow

the Chinaman through the streets, howling and scream-
ing after him to frighten him. They catch hold of his
queue, and pull him from his wagon. They throw brick-
bats and missiles at him, and so, often, this poor heathen
. . . reached his quarter of this Christian city covered
with wounds and bruises and blood. . . . Sometimes the
police have made a show of protecting the Chinaman,
but too frequently the effort has been a heartless one,
and the hoodlums have well understood their liberties
under our sacred guardians of law and order."

The roughneck attacks on the Chinese grew so vicious
that a group of citizens formed a Chinese Protective
Society in 1869. Members of this society met every
incoming ship to offer help to the arriving Chinese laborers. The society hired special policemen to guard the
Chinese immigrants on their first trip through San Francisco's streets from the docks to the Chinese quarters.
But many newspapers made fun of the organization,
calling it a "society for the prevention of cruelty to
Chinese." Lacking public support and money, the society
remained in operation only about one year.

Conditions grew worse for the Chinese in California
through the 1870s. Work on the transcontinental railroad ended. Many Californians thought that the Chinese
would be leaving in great numbers now that their services were no longer in great demand.

They guessed wrong. Though many Chinese did go
home, more came. Records of Chinese comings and
goings between 1868 and 1877, listed sixty thousand
leaving and 130,000 arriving.

As the Chinese population grew, many anti-Chinese groups were formed to work against Asian immigration —or against what these groups said was a "Yellow Peril" and the "Chinese menace." Accounts of eyewitnesses reported that "it was a common sight in San Francisco and other cities to see the Chinese pelted with stones or mud, beaten or kicked, having vegetables or laundry stolen from their baskets, and even having their queues cut." The most violent outbreak took place in 1871 in Los Angeles, which at that time was still a small town of just some six thousand people. There, a quarrel among the Chinese themselves brought a police raid on the Chinese quarters. During the raid, a policeman was wounded and a white civilian killed.

Rumors spread through town that the Chinese were "killing whites wholesale." These false reports brought an angry mob of whites storming into the Chinese quarters, burning and smashing as they went. Before the police regained control of the situation, at least eighteen Chinese had been lynched on the spot and many more injured. An investigation following the riots resulted in the trial and conviction of eight rioters. They received prison sentences ranging from two to six years. None of them, however, served their full terms. All were released from jail the following year.

At the same time the Chinese in San Francisco were being arrested in large numbers for violating some unusual local laws. The city politicians noted that Chinatown was jam-packed with people. On the excuse that overcrowding caused crime and disease, the city's Board of Supervisors passed a Cubic Air Ordinance. It said all adults must have at least five hundred cubic

Chinese laundrymen carried their wash in baskets suspended at the ends of long poles.

feet of living space. An unexpected problem arose, however, when the police began to drag Chinese out of
Chinatown by the carloads for violating the Cubic Air
Ordinance. The city jails became overfilled with Chinese
prisoners. The police found themselves breaking the law
for not giving each Chinese prisoner five hundred cubic
feet of jail space.

Along with the Cubic Air Ordinance came something
known as the Queue Ordinance. It said that all prisoners
in city jails had to have their hair cut within an inch of
their scalp. This, too, was supposed to be a health and
sanitation measure. However, few doubted that the real
reason for the ordinance was mainly to force the Chinese
to cut off their pigtails. A few of San Francisco's city
fathers and many local newspapers attacked the Queue
Ordinance. They felt it was a cruel and unusual punish-
ment directed against a single group of people. But the
Queue Ordinance remained on the books until it was
put to a court test in 1879.

A few years later came a laundry ordinance which
put a license fee of $2 every three months on laundries
using one-horse vehicles, $4 every three months on
laundries using two-horse vehicles, and $15 every three
months on laundries using *no* horse-drawn vehicles.
Chinese laundrymen at that time ordinarily could not
afford to keep a horse. They carried their wash Chinese-
style—in baskets suspended at the ends of long poles. By
setting the highest fee on horseless laundries, this license
law was clearly aimed at driving the Chinese out of
business.

The anti-Chinese movement reached a peak at a time when California went through one of its worst economic setbacks. Risky investments in silver mining stocks in neighboring Nevada's Comstock Lode had brought great wealth to a few. But most of the investors lost everything they had. In 1875, the Bank of California went broke, touching off a financial panic that shook California's economy from top to bottom.

In a time of fear and uncertainty, the anti-Chinese activities seemed to fuse in California's restless labor movement.

The favorite of the Workingmen's Party was an Irish firebrand named Denis Kearney, a soap-box orator who could whip crowds to a fever pitch of excitement. "And whatever happens," Kearney shouted, "the Chinese must go!" His sand lotters took these words for their battle cry.

Until the 1870s, the problem surrounding Chinese immigration to America was widely regarded as just a San Francisco problem, or a California problem, or at most a West coast problem. This was because the majority of the Chinese in America at that time settled in California—and mostly in the San Francisco area.

With the finishing of the transcontinental railroad, and with the depression and hard times in California, a trickle of Chinese immigrants began moving to other parts of the country: to the Pacific Northwest, to the Rocky Mountain states, and even to the eastern seaboard. For a while, there was some excitement in the South after the Civil War for using Chinese laborers to replace the freed Negro slaves in the cotton belt. But nothing much ever came of that idea.

The Chinese, because of different customs and ways of living, always seemed willing to work for minimum pay. This upset the newly organizing unions, such as the Knights of Labor. The unions feared that employers would hire the cheap foreign labor. If this happened, many American workingmen would be forced to accept lower pay if they wanted jobs. Wages for all American workingmen would go down.

These fears were partly brought out in 1870 during a strike for higher pay at a shoe factory in North Adams, Massachusetts. The factory owner not only refused the demands of the workers but also brought in two railroad carloads of Chinese laborers from the West coast. The Chinese strikebreakers took over the workers' jobs and the union strike failed. Similar events happened in Belleville, New Jersey, and Beaver Falls, Pennsylvania, all of which gave the national union organizations pause for second thought.

That such a situation could become explosive was borne out in 1885. Coal mines operated by the Union Pacific Railroad at Rock Springs, Wyoming, had 331 Chinese miners working there and 150 white miners. The white miners were members of the Knights of Labor. The Chinese were not. There had been no real effort to include the Chinese in the labor organization. For their part, the Chinese showed little interest in joining an American labor union.

The miners became divided into two distinct and mutually suspicious groups. Tensions between the two groups boiled over during an argument over which group was going to dig which face of what coal vein. The brawl turned into the Rock Springs Massacre of 1885.

A mob of over 150 white miners, many armed with Winchester carbines, killed twenty-eight Chinese miners, wounded fifteen, and chased the rest out of town. No casualty was reported among the whites.

In the days following the massacre, sixteen whites were arrested. But all were soon released. As the Grand Jury of Sweetwater County later reported: "We have diligently inquired into the occurrences at Rock Springs on the second day of September last, and though we have examined a large number of witnesses, no one has been able to testify to a single criminal act by any white person that day." The Grand Jury deeply regretted that, under these circumstances, it could not bring charges against any of the accused.

In the first one hundred years of United States history, the federal government took little action on immigration. The official position welcomed all immigrants who wished to come to the United States. In general, the federal government left the regulation of such immigration to the governments of each individual state.

On the matter of immigration from China, the federal government was further bound by the Burlingame Treaty signed by the United States and China in 1868. The treaty was the work of Anson Burlingame, onetime U. S. Congressman later appointed special envoy to the Chinese Imperial Court. Burlingame performed his duties with such skill that he soon won the admiration of the Chinese Emperor. In 1867, the Emperor invited Burlingame to serve the Chinese government as its envoy abroad. Burlingame accepted, and his major achievement in this post was the treaty that bore his name.

One part of the Burlingame Treaty specifically said that the Chinese had a right to be in America and Americans to be in China. It read: "The United States of America and the Emperor of China cordially recognized the inherent and inalienable right of man to change his home and allegiance, and also the mutual advantage of free immigration and emigration from one country to the other for purposes of curiosity, or travel, or as permanent residents." The treaty, however, did not give to the Chinese the privilege of becoming naturalized citizens of the United States.

Treaty or no treaty, pressures mounted on Congress to pass new laws regulating Chinese immigration. In 1878, Congress passed the Fifteen Passenger Bill. The bill limited each incoming trans-Pacific ship to carrying fifteen Chinese passengers, at the most. This they hoped would hold down the number of Chinese immigrants reaching U.S. shores. But President Rutherford B. Hayes refused to sign the Fifteen Passenger Bill. The President said that the United States had no right to break the Burlingame agreement without the approval of the Chinese government.

Next, Congress moved to change the provisions of the Burlingame Treaty. In 1880, a new agreement was made with the Chinese government giving the U.S. government the right to regulate, limit, and temporarily to stop Chinese immigration to America. But Chinese immigration was not to be absolutely stopped. For the new treaty applied mostly to unskilled Chinese manual laborers. It did not affect such groups as Chinese students coming to the United States to study.

Still, the 1880 U. S.-China Treaty gave the federal government the right to exercise strict control over Chinese immigration. Two years later Congress passed the Chinese Exclusion Act of 1882 stopping Chinese immigration for a ten-year period. When the first law expired in 1892, it was renewed for another ten years. Then, in 1902 and 1904, Congress passed new laws which, in effect, put Chinese exclusion on a permanent basis.

This was the first time the American government ever stopped people of a specific national origin from coming as immigrants to the United States. In the years following, small numbers of Chinese continued to make their way to America to stay here temporarily as students or short-term visitors of one kind or another. But for all practical purposes, no Chinese citizen could be legally admitted to the United States as an immigrant from 1882 until 1943, when the Chinese Exclusion Act was finally repealed.

CHAPTER NINE

WORLDS APART

"During their entire settlement in California, they (the Chinese) have never adapted themselves to our habits, mode of dress, or our education system . . . never ceased the worship of their idol gods, or advanced a step beyond the traditions of their native hive."

These words came from a report on Chinese immigration made in 1877 by the California Senate. Governors, congressmen, and newspapermen read the ten thousand copies that were printed. Some of the state senators were, among others, prejudiced and intolerant. They attacked the Chinese for failing to give up their old ways. It was the fact that the Chinese immigrant would not change his ways which angered and upset Americans.

He was separated by an ocean from home and family. Yet, the typical Chinese newcomer held on doggedly to his old-world loyalties and values. He changed very few of his Chinese habits and customs to fit his new life. He was a member of a group who stayed separated in most ways from the rest of America.

There were any number of reasons why the Chinese

in America stood off from the rest of America. One of the biggest problems was the shock of America on the newcomers from China. American way of life and thinking were totally unfamiliar. They were almost beyond understanding to many of the uneducated laborers who made up the main part of the Chinese immigrants. Most Chinese immigrants had a hard time learning the English language. Many could manage only a kind of pidgin English. The half-English, half-Cantonese sounds that came from their efforts to learn English only made them the butt of endless jokes.

There was an even more basic cause for the unwillingness of many Chinese immigrants to Americanize. It went back to the goals they had first set for themselves in coming to America. As we have already seen, few Chinese laborers came to California with the thought of staying for good. They came to find their fortunes. They hoped to get back home in the shortest time possible. Or as one Chinese immigrant put it at the time: "I have one foot in this country (the United States) and one foot . . . in China."

True, for many of them, their stay in America would turn out to be far longer than they had at first hoped. But in their minds, they remained *Gum San Hock*— "guests of the Golden Mountains." The Chinese' strong ties to their homeland did not end even on death. Most of them carefully made arrangements to see that, should they die while away from China, their bodies would be shipped back home for burial in their native homeland.

They continued to think of themselves as sojourners temporarily in America. As a result they saw no reason to change their old-world ways. Instead, they tried to

The sojourners tried to make their own Chinese-styled world in America.

make their own Chinese-styled world in America. They wanted a safe and familiar place in what was to them a strange and foreign land.

And when their presence in America began to cause trouble, the Chinese immigrants withdrew more and more into this tight little world of their own.

Wherever the Chinese gathered in large enough numbers in the frontier settlements and mining towns of the Old West, some member of the Chinese colony would soon make it his business to take care of the needs and wants of the rest of his group.

Quite likely, he would form a trading company, rent a small store, and begin selling Chinese groceries and supplies. Like many country stores, the shop was more than just a place of business. It was also a meeting place. Chinese for miles around would find their way to the store. There they would spend their spare time exchanging news and gossip with their countrymen while sitting around a warming stove.

If a Chinese shopkeeper was successful, his shop and services grew. He might hire a full time cook to operate a restaurant in an annex. Or he might set up a gambling hall for those of his countrymen who wanted to try their luck.

A shrine was sometimes built in a nearby log cabin to serve as a makeshift temple. Here, the immigrant miner could offer prayers to the gods of his homeland. These temples came to be known as "joss houses," a name thought to come from *Dios*, the Portuguese word for God.

The largest Chinese settlement on this side of the Pacific grew up in *Gum San Ta Foy*—the "big city of the Golden Mountains"—otherwise known as San Francisco. Almost all the Chinese immigrants at that time entered America through this seaport. And though Chinese centers would later grow in other major U.S. cities, San Francisco's Chinese quarters would long remain a kind of unofficial capital of the Chinese world in America.

"Little China," as it was called then, grew up in a twelve-block area. Pacific, California, Stockton, and Kearny streets made up its boundaries. Its main street has always been Dupont Street (though the street itself was later renamed Grant Avenue).

To many San Franciscans, Little China seemed almost like a piece of Canton which had been brought over from China and dropped in the middle of San Francisco. But there was nothing unusual about the architecture of the buildings in the Chinese district. Rather, it was a strange and exciting atmosphere created by the throngs of Chinese who walked its narrow streets and alleys. They went about their business as if they had never left their old country.

Chinatown played an important role in the life of the Chinese immigrant overseas. Within Chinatown, he was surrounded by people who spoke his language and understood his ways. It was here that the Chinese immigrant found a sense of security in a foreign land. Its theaters and restaurants, its gambling halls, pleasure palaces, and—too often, unfortunately, its opium parlors—offered a way of escaping, even for a little while, from the boredom, hard work, and loneliness of his work-filled life. It made him feel that he did not have to bother with the America outside of Chinatown.

For most of the Chinese, the endless routine of work from one day to the next was broken only by the yearly festivals sprinkled through the calendar year. As in their native China, the important holidays numbered six altogether: the New Year's Festival, three festivals honoring the dead, the Midautumn (or Moon) Festival, and the Dragon Boat Festival.

Of these, the New Year's Festival was by far the gayest and fanciest celebration of all. It marked the start of the new year by the lunar calendar used in China. This usually comes in late January or early February in the Western calendar. The first recorded Chinese New Year's celebration in America took place on February 1, 1851. And it soon became a yearly event in California's Chinese communities. The New Year was celebrated with all the time-honored pageantry of the original in China.

Regular work schedules were happily forgotten for the week-long New Year's festivities. Sometimes an entire company of miners left their cabins and claims to head for San Francisco for the holidays. There, they found a newly scrubbed Chinese quarters decorated with colorful lanterns. The narrow streets of Chinatown were filled with people decked out in their best and newest clothes.

They crowded into temples to offer a prayer for better things in the new year. They jammed the gaily decorated theaters to see actors in the familiar historical plays. They listened to musicians play high-pitched tunes punctuated by thumping drums and the clash of cymbals and gongs.

Every restaurant held its banquets. Tables were piled high with food for round after round of feasting. On New Year's Day, the celebrations were capped by traditional lion dances and dragon parades in Chinatown's streets. And through all of it, the Chinese quarters echoed with the sound of thousands of exploding firecrackers. As the *Daily Alta California* described it in 1858: "The Chinese throughout the state have been celebrating their New Year's Day with an energy which does them credit. The number of firecrackers burned and the quantity of noise and smoke let loose are beyond calculations."

The festivals were times for blowing off steam, for releasing bottled-up feelings. The Chinese sojourner in America tried to make the most of it. Well he might. For all too soon the holidays would end, and a tired sojourner would return to his everyday life of unending work and service.

Many Americans looked upon the life of the Chinese coolie as something on the level of slavery. But as we have seen earlier, most of the Chinese laborers who came to America did so of their own choice. They raised the money for the trip through some form of the credit-ticket system.

Under such a system, they were in debt to someone for the amount of money advanced to them for their trans-Pacific passage. To this could be added any additional debt and interest that they might have been charged for the loan. Once these debts were paid off through their earnings in the new country, they were—in theory, anyway—free to come and go as they pleased.

On New Year's Day, the celebrations were capped by traditional lion dances and dragon parades in Chinatown's streets.

In real life, however, most of these Chinese immigrants soon found themselves confused strangers in a foreign land. As strangers, they had little desire or chance to go their separate ways. They felt helpless in a new and difficult life. Many turned for direction and discipline to different Chinese associations that had been formed to offer protection for the individual Chinese. But, they also forced the Chinese to live by the associations' rules.

The old way of the Cantonese villages could be seen repeated again in America. For the most part, three associations were set up: the family associations, the district associations, and fraternal organizations that came to be called *tongs*.

The family associations, as you can tell by the name, took in all the members of the same family. For it was the custom for Chinese sojourners, once settled in a new country, to help other male relatives (brothers, cousins, nephews) to cross the ocean and find work. When enough of the relatives collected in one place, they formed associations or groups for protection and welfare. This set up the same tightly knit family structure as they had in old China. In the United States, however, the Chinese family associations were expanded to include all Chinese with the same family name, however distant the relationship between two Lees—or Wongs, Yees, Leongs, Chins, or whatever their names—might have been.

A second type of Chinese organization in America was the district associations, based not on family ties but on geographic ties. Chinese who came from the same home village, or home district, or in some cases the same group of home districts made up the district associations. The objectives of the district associations overlapped those of the family associations, and some of the Chinese immigrants joined both groups.

The trouble with this social setup was that it helped to continue in America the bad feelings found among different groups in China. Chinese who did not get along with one another in their native country found that their relations did not improve on this side of the Pacific. In effect, the Chinese brought their old-world feuds with them into the new world.

During the 1850s, rivalry between district associations touched off a series of Chinese wars in California's gold country. Battles were fought in Mariposa, El Dorado, Calaveras, Butte, Yuba, and Sierra counties. Even cities such as San Francisco and Sacramento witnessed an occasional fight between gangs of armed Chinese.

One district association would give a public challenge to another and soon the combat preparations were underway. For weeks the armies of the rival associations drilled and paraded. Blacksmith shops for miles around were kept busy hammering out swords, spears, pikes, and other weapons of war. Sometimes, muskets and bayonets were sent up from San Francisco.

On the appointed day, the rival forces faced each other across the battlefield, waving their banners and hurling insults at their opponents. Sometimes, local law officers appeared to stop the battles. Sometimes they did not—and a wild melee followed. Fortunately, the battles almost always ended quickly. The casualty counts were low—mercifully low, considering that hundreds of Chinese took part in these brawls.

By the 1860s, the district associations decided that there must be better ways to work out their problems than by fighting battles among themselves. Several of the district associations decided to join together to form a united organization. The number of member associations within the joint organization changed from time to time as some joined and others quit. But in its best days, the new organization had six major district associations so joined. It was then called the Chinese Six Companies in San Francisco, and the name stuck (later it became more formally known in English as the Consolidated Benevolent Association and in Chinese as the All China United Association).

The joint organizations were to settle arguments among different Chinese groups and to promote the welfare of all Chinese in America. Its activities ranged widely. It served as a pressure group to oppose laws which discriminated against the Chinese. It ran Chinese schools and hospitals and watched over Chinese employment and business dealings.

But the works and services performed by the Six Companies carried a price tag—a price tag counted not only in terms of dues, fees, and contributions required from its members, but also in terms of control over the individual immigrant. The Six Companies considered itself the spokesman for all the Chinese in America and expected all Chinese to obey its orders.

At the height of its powers in the 1860s and 1870s, it was an unofficial, yet effective, government which controlled the Chinese world in America.

The strongest challenge to the power and prestige of the Six Companies came from the third type of Chinese organization: the tongs.

Some of the tongs were exactly what they claimed to be—fraternal lodges organized only for social purposes. Other tong organizations, though, turned out to be just the opposite. They were vicious gangster brotherhoods which terrorized and victimized the Chinese communities in America.

The beginning of tongs is traced back to the secret societies in China. The tongs spent most of their time plotting the overthrow of the Imperial family then ruling over the Celestial Empire. But while the secret societies in China were mainly concerned with political rebellion, their offshoots in America seemed interested mainly in crime: murder, robbery, blackmail, extortion, kidnaping, and any other crimes that come to mind.

The criminal tongs of San Francisco began to grow in the 1880s and 1890s, partly by taking advantage of the conditions in Chinatown. During these years the mines were worked out and the railroad lines completed. Large numbers of unemployed Chinese laborers left the work camps of the California countryside and drifted into San Francisco. By 1875, the population of San Francisco's Chinatown swelled to about forty-seven thousand. But Chinatown's boundaries were not expanded to make room for the new residents. The result was horrible overcrowding. The living conditions were unbearable. Men were crammed into barracks-like rooms jammed with row after row of bunks.

Crime and vice thrived under the conditions of an overcrowded ghetto. Since the criminal tongs controlled

most of the illegal activities in Chinatown, they grew
fat off the profits.

Tong membership probably never numbered much
more than two or three thousand at its peak. The in-
fluence of the tongs depended less on number than
power. By threatening violence or death, they were able
to force the residents of Chinatown to do as they wished.
For this purpose each tong kept its own private army of
hired killers—"hatchet men" they were called because
they sometimes used hatchets (as well as knives, kitchen
cleavers, and revolvers) as tools of their murderous
trade.

The bloodiest clashes came when one tong fought
another tong. With armed cutthroats pitted against one
another, the struggle began to look like gangland warfare. Killing became such a cold-blooded business that
a wall at Dupont and Clay streets was called the mur-
derers' bulletin board. There, the tongs posted the
names of those marked for death. Next to the names
was the fee offered to any professional assassin willing
to undertake the job.

The San Francisco police occasionally cracked down
on the tongs with raids and mass arrests. But if such
tactics temporarily stopped tong wars, they had no last-
ing effect. Most people living in Chinatown did not
trust protection of American justice and feared tong
revenge. They, therefore, avoided co-operating with the
authorities. For their part, the police often took a toler-
ant view of the tongs so long as they fought their wars
within Chinatown and did not bother anyone outside
of it.

Tong crimes hurt the image of all the Chinese in America. The press printed lurid stories of tong warfare, just enough to lend some truth to a popular idea of Chinatown as a place where evil characters slinked through dark alleys bent on foul deeds. Visitors to San Francisco were solemnly warned against wandering around Chinatown alone and unprotected at night.

Ever so often, there were demands to do something about Chinatown. They ranged from cleaning it up to tearing it down. Editorials condemned Chinatown as a breeding place of crime, vice, and disease. Public demands called for resettling the Chinese outside San Francisco's city limits and urged the demolition of the Chinese quarters.

In the end, it was nature and not men which did the demolition job. The earth shook one April morning in 1906. Chinatown, and most of San Francisco, tumbled into ruin.

The first tremors were felt at 5:15 Wednesday morning, April 18, 1906. For 192 miles along an ancient fracture in the ground, called the San Andreas fault, the earth shifted. When the earthquake was over just forty-seven seconds later, the land on the western side of the rift had been moved sixteen feet north of where it had been.

In San Francisco, it was first heard as a low roar, then a louder rumble, and finally a series of explosive sounds. Pavements cracked and some streets sank. Buildings swayed. Walls and chimneys fell apart and tumbled to the ground.

Sleepy-eyed people, many barefoot and still dressed in night clothes, stumbled out of their houses and swarmed into the streets to find safety in the open areas.

The earthquake had overturned stoves, destroyed chimneys, snapped electrical wires and gas mains. Fires broke out all over the city, and firemen, to their horror, discovered that there was no water with which to fight the flames. The water mains were broken and useless. In desperation, city officials ordered buildings dynamited to create firebreaks. But the explosions only seemed to spread the flames.

By Wednesday evening, a solid wall of flames was sweeping through Chinatown, "scattering its inhabitants," author Charles Keeler reported, "in helpless bands. Out of the narrow alleyways and streets they swarmed like processions of black ants. With bundles swung on poles across their shoulders, they retreated, their helpless little women in pantaloons following with the children, all passive and uncomplaining. . . . In every quarter the night was full of terror. The mighty column of smoke rose thousands of feet in the air, crimsoned by the wild sea of flames below it."

For the next four days, the refugees huddled in temporary camps. They waited as fire swept back and forth across San Francisco. Before it all ended, 520 blocks of the city had been wiped clean by the flames, 28,188 buildings destroyed. The death toll was estimated at more than 450.

Chinatown was left totally in ashes, with only a few blackened walls of gutted buildings left standing. The old Chinatown was gone and the Chinese world in America would never quite be the same again—ever.

CHAPTER TEN

A NEW BEGINNING

In truth, many San Franciscans were not sorry to see old Chinatown destroyed. Even before the Great Fire was over, some of the city leaders were arguing against rebuilding Chinatown in the center of their city. They suggested that the Chinese be resettled in some other part of the city. If possible, they hoped the Chinese would settle outside the city limits altogether.

But if the Chinese themselves knew about such demands, they paid little attention to them. After the fire, they made their way back to the site of old Chinatown and began at once to rebuild. San Franciscans could do little about it, except to hope that a better Chinatown would rise out of the ashes.

This hope was one day realized, much to the relief and delight of San Francisco. The old Chinatown had been destroyed in the flames and was gone forever. In its place came a new, better looking Chinatown. To this day, it remains a featured attraction of San Francisco and a source of great pride to the city.

Changes taking place within the Chinese community in America could be seen in the new Chinatown. The Chinese made new efforts to win acceptance and a place of their own in the larger American community. In that sense, the great earthquake and fire of 1906 marked a major turning point in the story of the Chinese people in America.

The changes, of course, did not take place in a few days or a few weeks, or in just a year or two. The changes came slowly, over many years and generations. Some of these changes can be seen only by taking a long look backward in time.

The Chinese in America during the 19th century were men without roots. They were a society of sojourners, men who did not intend to stay here. It was a community in which men greatly outnumbered women and bachelors far outnumbered family men. In short, it did not have the closely tied family groups which played such an important role in their life before coming to America.

Time itself worked changes in the makeup of this community of Chinese overseas. Between 1870 and 1920, many thousands of bachelors returned to China. Other thousands died here. In that fifty-year period, the recorded Chinese population in the United States dropped from 107,000 to 61,000.

Survival of the Chinese community in America depended on those Chinese who, at some point, decided that they would stay and settle in the United States and bring up families here. As family life returned, many of the problems that had long plagued the old, rootless Chinese community—from tong wars to opium smoking—began to disappear.

These changes brought a new kind of person: the Chinese-American—or, more properly, the American of Chinese ancestry. His birth in this country automatically made him a U.S. citizen. Although he is proud of his Chinese background, this American tends to identify with the country of his birth rather than with the homeland of his forebears. (It should be pointed out that the term "Chinaman," once freely used to describe a Chinese or a person of Chinese ancestry, is no longer acceptable. The Chinese consider the term highly insulting.)

The change from one culture to another did not always take place easily or smoothly. Many Americans with Chinese parents felt the tug between two cultures— Chinese and American. They sometimes felt that they fully belonged to neither group. Still, bit by bit, each new generation of Chinese-Americans became more Americanized and less Chinese than the one before. The old attitudes that made Chinatown a separate community within a larger community slowly gave way. In an atmosphere of growing tolerance, understanding, and opportunity, Chinese-Americans began to take part more and more in American life.

In the process, they have enriched American life (as witness the popularity of Chinese food and the ever-present Chinese-American restaurants). In ways large and small, individual Chinese-Americans have contributed to American science, to business and industry, to architecture, the arts and letters. Perhaps the biggest contribution of Chinese-Americans has come in the field of American education. Hundreds of Chinese-American teachers and professors now serve on the staffs of our schools and universities.

And in this way the Chinese-American is emerging as a recognizable person, no longer content to be just one more face in a Chinese crowd. It is a search for his individual identity which had begun when his fore-bears first made the passage across the Pacific to the Golden Gate—more than a hundred years ago.

INDEX